W9-DGN-164

PHONICS

for the Teacher of Reading

Second Edition

Programmed for Self-Instruction

PHONICS
for the Teacher of Reading
Second Edition

MARION A. HULL

Charles E. Merrill Publishing Company
A Bell & Howell Company
Columbus, Ohio

Published by
Charles E. Merrill Publishing Company
A Bell & Howell Company
Columbus, Ohio 43216

This book was set in Univers.
The Production Editors were Susan Sylvester-Glick and Michael Robbins.
The cover was designed by Will Chenoweth.

International Standard Book Number: 0-675-08655-8
Library of Congress Catalog Card Number: 75-21172
3 4 5 6 7 8 9 10 — 80 79 78

Printed in the United States of America

PREFACE

This text is designed for the person who is teaching or intends to teach reading to children. It is programmed for self-instruction so that its user may work individually, at his own rate of speed, to acquire the background in phonics essential to a teacher of reading.

It must be emphasized that this program in *no way* proposes a method or sequence for the teaching of phonics skills to children, nor does it dictate the content to be taught. The aim, in its preparation, was to provide a depth of knowledge to give the teacher a feeling of security in using any materials and any method related to this phase of the total reading program. This approach required the introduction of terminology and concepts beyond that needed by children.

Is there a need for a programmed text in phonics? In recent years, phonics has received much attention, not only in the literature—newspapers, popular magazines, educational books, and journals—but also within reading programs, those designed to teach reading through the phonics approach as well as the revised versions of standard basic texts and the new linguistic readers.

Many a lay person has been led to believe that phonics has not been a part of the school's reading program since the early 1900s. Anyone who has examined reading instructional materials knows that this is not true. For decades, the basal readers, as well as the teacher's manuals and workbooks, have made systematic presentations of phonics as part of the word attack skills to be mastered. Since these basal readers have been the chief means of teaching reading, why do so many adults—including college students—maintain that they have never had instruction in phonics? Why are children not more capable when encountering new words?

Is it possible that, although the reading programs contain phonics, the teachers ignore it, that they teach phonics only when they approach the teaching of reading with materials that are completely phonics-oriented? If this is the case, why is it so? A plausible reason is that the teacher does not have an adequate personal background in phonics. Various studies[*] give evidence that this assertion is true. These studies indicate that the teacher's knowledge of phonics increases little by taking college courses in the teaching of reading.

It may well be that a more adequate job is not done in the reading methods courses because it is such a time-consuming task. The prospective teacher must develop methods for teaching the word attack skills, to say nothing of developing his own background of phonics knowledge. The college teacher, faced with instructing the student in the methods of teaching phonics, soon discovers that such instruction can consume all the time to be spent on this phase of the reading course. As a result, the professor may assign one of the excellent books on the subject for independent study. It appears, however, that this is inadequate. It is like asking a student to read an algebra book. To learn phonics, one must work at it, not simply read about it.

How does one work at it? Phonics is a subject which lends itself to programming for self-instruction. With the subject matter broken down into discrete steps which a student can work through on his own, at his own speed, outside the class period, receiving reinforcement and encountering structured review in the process, the solution appears to have been found. It is for this purpose that this text was written.

In view of the inconsistencies in the English language, the variations in regional pronunciation, and the inconclusiveness of research on the relative usefulness of specific generalizations, it was necessary to make some arbitrary decisions regarding the phonics content to be included. Whenever applicable, *The American College Dictionary*[†] served as the basis for decisions. Teachers of foreign language speaking children and children who speak other than a more or less "standard English" will need to supplement their study with books pertaining to the particular needs.

I wish to express appreciation to my former colleagues at Northern Illinois University and to the many students who, by field testing the program, have assisted in its development.

M.A.H.

---

[*]Albert J. Mazurkiewicz, "What Do Teachers Know About Phonics," *Reading World*, XIV (1975), 165-77.

[†]*The American College Dictionary.* C. L. Barnhart, Editor-in-Chief. (New York: Random House, 1970).

TO THE STUDENT

What kind of background do you have in the phonics needed for teaching reading to children? To help determine the depth of your present knowledge or lack of knowledge and to aid in evaluating your growth, this text includes a pretest and a posttest. Do not examine the posttest until you have completed this programmed text. Turn to page 1 and take the pretest now. Correct it. At your next sitting, turn back to this section and continue reading.

Read these directions carefully. The success of your study depends chiefly on two factors: (1) your desire to obtain a background in phonics to aid you in teaching reading to children; (2) the care with which you follow these directions as you proceed through this program.

The program is arranged in frames. Each frame requires a response. The left portion of the frame indicates the expected response. It is absolutely essential that you write your response *before* you see this expected response. To avoid glancing at the left column, cut the mask from the back cover of this book or make one of heavy paper. Place the mask over the left-hand column to conceal the correct response.

When you have studied and written your response to the first frame, move the mask down to reveal the answers to that frame. Compare your answer with the expected answer. Since this is a teaching device (not a test) and is designed to guide you to the correct responses, you will more than likely find that you have the correct answer. If you do not, study the material again. Write the correct response. Equivalent answers may be considered correct; make sure that they are equivalent.

You will find that there is much repetition and review. This will help you fix the important points in mind. It may seem that you are asked to make simple, obvious answers. You may be tempted not to write them and instead to respond mentally or look at the answers while your are reading the frame. *THIS WILL DEFEAT THE PURPOSE OF THE PROGRAM* and will be a waste of your time. It is essential that you make the written response or responses to the entire frame before you see the answers.

Do not work too long at one sitting; one-half hour to forty-five minutes is a good study period for this program. Several periods in one day will prove to be better than one long period. Arrange your study so that you will be able to keep an active mind.

Now cover the left-hand column of the first page. Study the first frame. Make the required response. (In this case you will select the correct word from the two choices under the blank.) Move the mask down to reveal the answers to the first frame. Compare the two so that your learning is immediately reinforced. If your answer is correct, study the second frame. Fill in the blank. If you read the first frames with an active mind, you will make the correct answers. If you are incorrect, review; then write the correct answers. Proceed through the following frames in a similar fashion.

Turn to page 7.

CONTENTS

Self-evaluation I: A Pretest

This is a test designed to give an indication of your present knowledge in the field of phonics. Read each item, including <u>all</u> the choices. Indicate the answer you consider best by circling the appropriate letter (a, b, c, d, or e) or marking the appropriate letter on an answer sheet. Be sure to respond to every item. Time: 30 minutes

I. Multiple Choice. Select the best answer.

1. A requirement of a syllable is that
   a. it contain at least one consonant letter.
   b. it contain no more than one vowel letter.
   c. it be a pronounceable unit.
   d. it contain no more than one phoneme.
   e. All of the above

2. Which of the following most adequately completes the sentence? All the consonant speech sounds in the American-English language are represented by
   a. the distinctive speech sounds we associate with the 21 consonant letters of the alphabet.
   b. 18 of the consonant letters of the alphabet plus certain digraphs.
   c. the single letter consonants plus their two- and three-letter blends.
   d. the consonant-vowel combinations.
   e. The American-English language is too irregular to represent the consonant speech sounds with any degree of accuracy.

3. The letter *y* is most likely to be a consonant when
   a. it is the first letter in a word or syllable.
   b. it is the final letter in a word or syllable.
   c. it follows *o* in a syllable.
   d. it has the sound of *i* as in *might*.
   e. None of the above.

4. Generally, when two like-consonants appear together in a word,
   a. only one is sounded.
   b. one is sounded with the first syllable and the other with the second.
   c. both are sounded when the preceding vowel is *i*.
   d. both are sounded when the following vowel is *e*.
   e. Neither is sounded

5. The second syllable of the nonsense word *alithpic* would be expected to rhyme with
   a. aright.
   b. brick.
   c. kith.
   d. pyth (as in python).
   e. hit.

6. The open syllable of the nonsense word *botem* would most likely rhyme with
   a. coat.
   b. hot.
   c. rah.
   d. low.
   e. gem.

7. A diphthong is best illustrated by the vowels representing the sound of
   a. *ow* in *snow*.
   b. *ou* in *mouse*.
   c. *oo* in *foot*.
   d. *ai* in *said*.
   e. a. and b.

8. The sound of the schwa is represented by
   a. the *a* in *baited*.
   b. the *e* in *early*.
   c. the *i* in *pencil*.
   d. the *w* in *show*.
   e. All of these

9. How many phonemes are represented in *knight*?
   a. one   b. two   c. three   d. four   e. six

10. An example of a closed syllable is
    a. desk.
    b. home.
    c. tight.
    d. All of these
    e. None of these

11. The consonant blend is illustrated by
    a. the *sh* in *shirt*.
    b. the *ng* in *thing*.
    c. the *ph* in *graph*.
    d. the *br* in *brought*.
    e. a., c., and d.

12. Which of the following has the incorrect diacritical mark?

    a. cǎll   b. sĕll   c. ĭll   d. hŏt   e. ŭp

13. Which of the following has an incorrect diacritical mark?

    a. māde   b. sēe   c. tīme   d. lōve   e. ūse

14. When the single vowel *i* in an accented syllable is followed by a single consonant and a final *e*, the *i* would most likely have the sound of

    a. the *i* in *active.*

    b. the *y* in *my.*

    c. the *i* in *easily.*

    d. the first *e* in *bee.*

    e. None of the above

15. If *o* were the only and final vowel in an accented syllable, that *o* would most likely represent the same sound as

    a. the *o* in *nothing.*

    b. the *a* in *wanted.*

    c. the *o* in *do.*

    d. the *ew* in *sew.*

    e. None of these

16. The letter *q* could be removed from the alphabet because it could adequately and without conflict be represented by

    a. the "soft sound of *c.*"

    b. *ch* as in *choir.*

    c. *k* as in *keep.*

    d. All of the above

    e. The idea is foolish; *qu* represents a distinctive consonant sound.

17. If *a* were the single vowel in an accented syllable ending with one or more consonants, that *a* would most likely represent the same sound as

    a. the *ai* in *plaid.*

    b. the *ay* in *ray.*

    c. the *a* in *all.*

    d. the *a* in *any.*

    e. None of these

18. When *oa* appear together in a syllable, they usually represent the same sound as

    a. the *o* in *bottle.*

    b. the *o* in *orb.*

    c. the *o* in *toil.*

    d. the *o* in *come.*

    e. None of these

19. The symbol *s* is used in the dictionary to show the pronunciation of the sound heard in

    a. shall   b. his   c. sugar   d. seem   e. b. and d.

20. If *e* were the only vowel in an open syllable, the *e* would most likely represent the same sound as

    a. the *e* in *pine.*

    b. the *ea* in *meat.*

    c. the *y* in *my.*

    d. the *e* in *set.*

    e. None of these

21. The word *if* ends with the same sound as
    a. the *ph* in *graph.*
    b. the *f* in *of.*
    c. the *gh* in *taught.*
    d. the *gh* in *ghetto.*
    e. a. and b.

22. The letter *c* followed by *i* is most likely to represent the same sound as
    a. the *s* in *sent.*
    b. the *c* in *cello.*
    c. *c* followed by *o.*
    d. *c* followed by *e.*
    e. Both a. and d.

23. The letter *g* followed by *o* is most likely to represent the same sound as
    a. the *j* in *joke.*
    b. the *g* in *ghost.*
    c. the *g* in *swing.*
    d. *g* followed by *e.*
    e. Both a. and d.

II. Multiple Choice. Where does the accent fall in the words or nonsense words given at the left? Indicate your answer by selecting the last two letters of the accented syllable found in the same row as the word.

Look at the example: *showboat.* The first "word" in a compound word is generally accented: *show'boat.* Look for the last two letters of *show, ow,* in the row to the right. You would circle b. or mark b. on your answer sheet.

Example:
    showboat   a. ho   (b.) ow   c. bo   d. at

24.	contract (noun)	a. co	b. on	c. nt	d. ra	e. ct
25.	frottomly	a. ro	b. ot	c. to	d. om	e. ly
26.	plargain	a. la	b. ar	c. rg	d. ga	e. in
27.	desridly	a. de	b. es	c. ri	d. id	e. ly
28.	cidaltion	a. ci	b. id	c. da	d. al	e. on
29.	phight	a. hi	b. ig	c. gh	d. ht	

III. Complete each sentence by selecting the word for which the correct pronunciation is indicated.

30. I went to the park for a
    a. pĭc'nĭc   b. wôk   c. rəst   d. pär'tē   e. rĭde

31. When I picked my vegetables, I dropped a
    a. lĕt'ĭs lēv   b. kūk'ŭm bər   c. kăr'ŏt   d. kăb'ĭg   e. bēt

32. The tree we planted was a
    a. pälm   b. wĭl'ou   c. mā̄p'le   d. kŏt'ən wŭd   e. sĭk'ə mōr

33. I went to the men's store to get (a)
    a: sŏgz   b. shōōz   c. trou'sərs   d. chərt   e. nək tī'

34. The wall is
    a. krăkt   b. smōōth   c. rôf   d. pānt əd'   e. thĭk

35. The committee was composed of
    a. klûr'gĭ mĕn   b. loi'ərz   c. băngk'ərz   d. te'zhərs   e. jŭd'jĭs

IV. Multiple Choice. Select the word in each row which is <u>incorrectly</u> syllabicated.

36. a. ro bot   b. ro bin   c. ro bust   d. ro tor   e. rouge

37. a. let hal   b. rab bit   c. dras tic   d. mer cy   e. con nect

38. a. un der line   b. un e qual   c. un ite   d. pre dic a ment   e. re mit

39. a. home work   b. book man   c. eye ball   d. now here   e. egg nog

V. Multiple Choice. There are three "words" in each item (a, b, c). Select the word or nonsense word in which you would hear the same sound as that represented by the underlined part of the word at the left. You may find that the sound is heard in all three words; if so, mark d. If none of the words contain the sound, mark e.

Nonsense words (indicated by asterisks) follow the generalizations of phonics or the common pattern.

40.	mention	a. special	b. sugar	c. machine	d. All	e. None
41.	the	a. thistle	b. mother	c. think	d. All	e. None
42.	jet	a. gnome	b. gisen*	c. sang	d. All	e. None
43.	into	a. thick	b. watch	c. hoped	d. All	e. None
44.	success	a. adceon*	b. kneo*	c. queer	d. All	e. None
45.	home	a. honor	b. night	c. who	d. All	e. None
46.	tall	a. talk	b. fault	c. gnaw	d. All	e. None
47.	food	a. look	b. blood	c. bought	d. All	e. None
48.	boil	a. mouse	b. employ	c. riot	d. All	e. None
49.	would	a. whom	b. once	c. cow	d. All	e. None
50.	sang	a. ranger	b. ponder	c. thinker	d. All	e. None

(See the Appendix for answers to Self-Evaluation I)

Number correct _____

I. Introduction

Place a mask over the left-hand column. Study the first frame where a choice of two words is offered. Select the correct word and fill in the blank. Move the mask down to the first horizontal line below the frame. Compare your response with that given in the left-hand column across from the blank. If your answer does not agree with the one at the left, restudy the frame and then write the correct response. Study the second frame. Supply the correct word for the blank. Move the mask down and compare responses. Continue in this fashion, never moving the mask until you have made a response. Always complete the entire frame before moving the mask.

spoken	1. The language of any people is the sound system by which the individuals communicate with one another. The written language is merely a system of <u>symbols</u> used to represent the _____ language. (written, spoken)
symbols (or code)	2. Reading, in an oversimplified sense, is decoding. In other words, reading is translating the _____ into the correct speech sounds.
phoneme	*phoneme* *grapheme* 3. The suffix *eme* denotes a basic structural element of a language. *Phon* (tele<u>phone</u>, <u>phono</u>graph, etc.) refers to voice or sound. One speech sound is called a _____ (*phon* + *eme*).

sound	4. These word-pairs illustrate the definition of a phoneme. As you pronounce each pair, notice the sound which makes the top word different from the one beneath it. *pin* *pin* *pin* *pin* *tin* *pen* *pit* *chin* A phoneme is the smallest unit of _____ which distinguishes one word from another.
t	5. To attain a better understanding of a phoneme, let's examine these words more closely. How does *pin* differ from *tin*? *pin* *tin* The sounds represented by the *p* and the _____ are the smallest units of sound which distinguish *pin* from *tin*.
sound *i, e*	6. Compare the phonemes represented by the underlined letters in the set of words at the right. *pin* *pen* Remember that the phoneme is a _____, so say the words aloud. The sounds which are represented by the _____ and the _____ are the smallest units which distinguish *pin* from *pen*.
n, t	7. Pronounce the words at the right. The sounds which are represented *pin* by the _____ and the _____ are the smallest units which distinguish *pin* *pit* from *pit*.
grapheme	8. Sounds cannot be written! Letters do not speak! We use a letter or letters to represent a phoneme. "*Graph*" means "drawn, written, recorded." The _____ (*graph* + *eme*) is the written representation of the phoneme.
p i n *p i n*	9. When you say the word *pin*, you hear three phonemes. We represent these three phonemes with the letters _____ _____ _____. In other words, the three graphemes in *pin* are _____ _____ _____.
phonemes one	10. When you say the word *chin*, you hear three _____. *pin* *Ch* represents one speech unit; you cannot divide it. Since the grapheme is the written representation of the phoneme, *ch* is also *chin* _____ grapheme. (How many?)

ch i *n*	11. We represent the three phonemes in *chin* with the graphemes _____ _____ _____.
ch	12. We represent the first phoneme in the word *chart* with the grapheme _____.
phoneme	13. A grapheme is the written symbol of the _____. It may be composed of one or more letters.
grapheme phoneme graphemes *k, c, q*	14. The phoneme is a speech sound. The _____ is composed of the symbols we use to picture the sound on paper. *keep* *come* Say the words at the right. In each one you will hear the *quit* _____ which we commonly associate with the underlined letter. Three different _____ are used to represent this phoneme. They are _____, _____, and _____.
3, 3 *w, a* *tch, tch*	15. Grapheme and letter are not synonymous. A grapheme never consists of less than a letter, but it may consist of more than one letter. The grapheme represents the phoneme. Examine the word *watch*. *w a tch* Say it out loud. It is composed of _____ phonemes. Therefore, it is composed of _____ graphemes—one grapheme to represent each phoneme. The graphemes are _____, _____, and _____. What letters represent the final grapheme of the word *watch?* _____
phonemes (or speech sounds)	16. Although there are hundreds of different speech sounds (consider the variations due to dialect, individual speech patterns, change in stress, etc.), for all practical purposes in the task of teaching reading, we can consider the American-English language to contain 44 separate _____.
phoneme letter	17. If there were a one-to-one correspondence between letter and phoneme (that is, if we had one letter for each _____ and one phoneme for each _____), the task of teaching children to read would be much simpler than it now is.
26 phonemes	18. The truth is that we have only _____ letters in our alphabet, only 26 symbols to represent 44 _____.

phonemes	19. We add symbols to our system by using combinations of letters (such as *ch, th*) to represent the _____ not represented by the 26 letters of the alphabet.
phoneme, *a*	20. We also add symbols by using one letter to represent more than one _____. (The letter _____, for example, represents 3 different phonemes in the 3 words *ate, pan, all.*)
letter (or symbol or grapheme)	21. Sometimes when a letter represents more than one phoneme, there are clues within the word to indicate which sound the _____ represents. A teacher of reading should be able to recognize these clues.
gh, ph phoneme	22. Besides lacking a one-to-one correspondence between the letters of the alphabet and the phonemes needed, the spelling of the English language is further complicated by its many inconsistencies. One of the greatest of these is the use of different symbols to represent the same phoneme. For example, the sound we associate with *f* is represented by *f* in *fine,* by _____ in *cough,* and by _____ in *elephant*. This is an example of 3 graphemes representing one _____.
phonemes	23. There are, in fact, 251 different ways to spell the _____ of which our spoken language is composed. (letters, phonemes)
graphemes phonemes	24. In other words, there are 251 _____ to represent the 44 (graphemes, phonemes) _____. (graphemes, phonemes)
k, g, h	25. Another of the many complications is the use of symbols which do not represent any sound: *knight* has three letters which do not represent sound—the _____, _____, and _____.
phonemes sound (or phoneme)	26. We have noted that the alphabet is a symbolic representation of our speech sounds (or _____), that there is not a one-to-one correspondence between the symbol and the _____, and that there are many inconsistencies in the symbolic system.

letters (Phoneme is in-
correct; this refers to
letters, not sounds.)

27. However, there are certain symbols which are reliable and there are patterns of reliability within the inconsistencies. The teacher of reading must be aware of these. It is the purpose of this program to aid you in your understanding of one of the sets of skills of word recognition, the phonics skills.

We shall begin our study with the most reliable of the 26 _____ of the alphabet, the consonants.

II. Consonants

Place the mask over the left-hand column. As you work through these sections, it will be necessary for you to make sounds out loud. Be sure that you are seated where this is possible. Now work out the first frame, move the mask down to check and proceed as you did in the first section. Keep an active mind! You may need to study the entire frame before you make your response.

vowels	1. The 26 letters of the alphabet can be divided into two major categories: consonants and _____ .
consonants	2. There is, however, a degree of overlapping between these categories. Certain letters, notably the *w* and *y*, sometimes function as vowels and at other times as _____ .
consonants, 21	3. Recognizing the fact that we are oversimplifying the situation, we shall, in this part of the program, consider all letters except *a, e, i, o, u* to be _____ . There are then _____ consonant letters. (How many?)
is not	4. We have noted previously that in the American-English language there _____ a one-to-one correspondence between letter and phoneme. (is, is not) Let us now see how this applies to consonants.

21, 25
 	
is not
	5. There are (for our purposes in the teaching of reading) 44 phonemes, 25 of these being consonant phonemes.
	
	There are _____ consonant letters; _____ consonant phonemes.
	     (How many?) (How many?)
	
	There _____ one letter for each phoneme.
	        (is, is not)

letter is not	6. Not only are there more phonemes than letters, but there are also some inconsistencies: some letters are used to represent more than one sound; certain sounds are represented by more than one _____. It is clear that there _____ a one-to-one correspondence between con- (is, is not) sonant phoneme and consonant letter.
yes	7. The phonemes of our language are very familiar to us, but to prepare ourselves to teach others to read, it is necessary to identify each of the 44 phonemes. Since there is not a one-to-one correspondence between sound and letter, it will be helpful to designate a key symbol for each phoneme. In this way we will know the sound to which we are referring no matter how it is represented in the word (that is, no matter how it is spelled). Whenever possible, the key symbol will be the same as the letter we ordinarily associate with the sound. For example, *b* will serve as the key symbol for the sound we hear at the beginning of the word *box*. Would you expect *d* to serve as the key symbol for the sound heard at the beginning of the word *dog*? _____
44, 25 phonemes (or sounds) (If you said letters, reread frame 7.)	8. There are 44 phonemes; 25 of these are consonant phonemes. We will, therefore, identify _____ key symbols altogether, of which _____ will be (How many?) (How many?) consonants. There will be a one-to-one correspondence between key symbols and _____.
symbol letter *bomb*	9. Most of the consonants are reliable with respect to sound. Therefore, in most cases, the key _____ which designates a certain phoneme heard in a word will be the same as the consonant _____ seen in that word. For example, *b* will serve as the key symbol for the initial sound we hear in the word _____. (*bomb, mob*)

No (The final *b* represents no phoneme: it is a silent letter.)	10. Will *b* serve as the key symbol for the final sound we hear in the word *bomb*? _____
4, 4 *g, r, a, ph* *f*	11. The word *graph* has _____ phonemes and therefore _____ graphemes. (How many?) (How many?) They are _____, _____, _____, and _____. So that we have a clue to its pronunciation, the logical key symbol to assign to the final phoneme in *graph* is the letter _____.
ph *f*	12. Pronounce *phrase.* The initial grapheme is _____. The key symbol to represent this sound is _____.
key symbols	13. We can divide the 25 consonant phonemes into two major groups: (1) Eighteen consonant phonemes identified by key symbols composed of single letters. (2) Seven consonant phonemes identified by _____ _____ composed of two-letter combinations. There will be a third group: the letters which represent no phonemes, the silent letters.

REVIEW 1

This review should give you some indication of the effectiveness of your study. Strive to fill in all the blanks without looking back. If you don't suceed, analyze your study procedure. Is your mind active? Are you writing all the answers? Do you complete a frame before you move the mask down? Try summarizing your learnings before you start the review. Complete the entire review before you check your answers.

1. Is there a one-to-one correspondence between the consonant letters and the consonant phonemes?

_____

2. We shall learn to identify a key symbol for each of the consonant _____ of the American-
                                                              (letters, phonemes)
English language.

3. The *m* is a very dependable letter, it is the key symbol for the initial sound heard in *man*. We would expect the key symbol representing the sound heard at the end of the word *jam* to be _____.

4. Dictionaries also use _____ as the key symbol to represent the sound heard at the beginning of the word *man.*

5. Most of the key symbols will be single letters; however, seven of the consonant symbols will be composed of _____ letters.

6. We can divide the consonant phonemes into two groups according to whether the key symbol representing the phoneme is composed of one or of two _____.

7. When a consonant letter appears in a word but represents no phoneme at all, we call it a _____ letter.

(For Answers to the Reviews, see the Appendix, page 113.)

s/z, f/v

	s (sat) *z (zoo)*
	1. The first consonant phoneme we shall consider is that heard at the beginning of the word *sat*. Say *sat* out loud. Now start to say *sat* and hold the first sound. Continue to hold it while you note the position of your lips, teeth, and tongue. Of course, the breath to make the sound comes through the throat, but notice that the sound originates in the mouth, not in the vocal cords. It is called <u>voiceless</u>.
	Place your hand closely around your throat with your thumb and forefinger against your jawbone. Now "slide" from the sound we shall identify by the key symbol *s* to that heard at the beginning of *zoo*. (This exercise will not make sense if you do not make the sounds aloud.) Feel the vibration of your vocal cords as you hold the <u>voiced</u> sound identified by the key symbol *z*.
yes (If you said "no," repeat the above activity.)	Can you make this pair of sounds without changing the position of your lips, teeth, and tongue? _____
voiceless	2. The *s* represents more of a whispered phoneme; we call it _____. (voiced, voiceless)
voiced	Its counterpart (or pair), the *z*, represents a <u>v_____</u> phoneme because it is pronounced while vibrating the vocal cords. Say the sound represented by the *s* again. Prolong the sound, then "add voice" (that is, slide the voiceless sound into a voiced sound). It has now become the sound repre-
z	sented by the letter _____.
	3. When we use the *s* as a key symbol in this program, we will be referring to one and only one of the 44 phonemes.
voiceless	This is the <u>v_____</u> sound we hear at the beginning of *sat*. When we use *z* as a key symbol, we will be referring to one, and only one, of the 44
phonemes, voiced	_____ of the American-English language. This is the <u>v_____</u> sound we hear at the beginning of the word *zoo*.

c	4. Let's make sure we understand the significance of the above. The key symbol *s* identifies one phoneme, but this phoneme is represented by at least <u>six</u> graphemes. In other words, we use six different spellings to stand for the sound we hear at the beginning of the word *sat.* Study the words at the right. The phoneme we represent by the key symbol *s* is <u>heard</u> in each of these words, but the letter *s* does <u>not appear</u> in any of them. *city* *receive* *bicycle* In each case the sound is represented by the grapheme _____. (What letter?)
sity *reseive* *bisycle* *s*	5. Rewrite the words at the right, substituting the key symbol *s* for the letter which represents the *s* phoneme. (Think of yourself as making dictionary clues to pronunciation.) Test each word to see if it has the sound which you hear at the beginning of the word *sat.* *city* _____ *receive* _____ *bicycle* _____ You have indicated that sound by using the key symbol _____.
rise *sene* *mis* *some* *sism* *s*	6. Rewrite the words at the right, substituting the key symbol *s* for the underlined parts. Pronounce the words you have written. The underlined part (the grapheme) in each of the words at the right represents the sound to which we have assigned the key symbol _____. *rice* _____ *scene* _____ *miss* _____ *some* _____ *schism* _____
s *s* *z*	7. Pronounce the words at the right. Listen very carefully to the underlined part. Which key symbol represents each part? Write it in the space following the word. To test, try both the voiced and voiceless phoneme. *hiss* _____ *history* _____ *his* _____
   soap, ask *rose, his* *sure, sugar* *measure, treasure*	8. We have noted that we use several different graphemes (*c, sc,* etc.) to represent the phoneme we identified by the key symbol *s.* The grapheme *s* is used to represent different phonemes also. Study the words at the right. The single consonant *s* represents the sound we usually associate with *s* in the words _____ and _____ with *z* in the words _____ and _____ with *sh* in the words _____ and _____ with *zh* in the words _____ and _____ *soap* *ask* *rose* *his* *sure* *sugar* *measure* *treasure*

z voiced, z	9. Pronounce *his* and *has* aloud. The key symbol which represents the final sound in these words is _____. There are many words in which the grapheme *s* actually represents its v_____ counterpart, the _____.

z   z *(toyz)*
    z *(dogz)*
    z *(bedz)*
    s *(cats)*
    s *(tops)*
z, z   *(houzez)*
	10. In many plural endings, when the preceding phoneme is voiced, we use the voiced sound whose key symbol is _____. *toy* _____
	
	dog _____
	Write the key symbol for each of the plural endings of the words at the right. Vowels and *g* and *d* are voiced; *t* and *p* are voiceless. *bed* _____
	        cat _____
	
	     top _____
	Note what happens to *house: house: house, hou_e_*

sizorz *zerxez* *fizle* *us* *fuze*	11. Rewrite the words at the right using the key symbol which represents the sound of each underlined part. Say each word aloud so that you can hear which are voiceless and which have "the voice added." Prolong the consonant sound: vowel phonemes are always voiced and may confuse you if you add the vowel sound to the consonant sound. *scissors* _____ *Xerxes* _____ *fizzle* _____ *us* _____ *fuse* _____
puzlez *lesonz* *glasez*	12. Perhaps you feel that you should use the key symbol twice for fizzle. Try pronouncing it with two phonemes represented by the *z*. (One *z* does it, doesn't it?) Write these words using key symbols to represent the sounds of the underlined graphemes. *puzzles* _____ *lessons* _____ *glasses* _____
rugz, iz, doez *peaz, some, pleazhure* *whoze, so, shurely*	13. Rewrite the following words using *s, z, sh,* or *zh* to indicate the sound the *s* represents: *rugs* _____ *is* _____ *does* _____ *peas* _____ *some* _____ *pleasure* _____ *whose* _____ *so* _____ *surely* _____

s, sat	14. When we see an *s* in an unknown word, we have few clues to tell us which phoneme it represents. We might note:
	(1) The letter *s* usually represents the sound we associate with the key symbol _____. It is the sound heard in _____. *(sat, sure)*
moss	(2) Except for certain foreign names (as *Saar*), the *s* at the beginning of a word stands for the sound heard in _____. *(moss, whose)*
z voiced	(3) We tend to use the phoneme represented by the voiced counterpart of *s* (the _____) for plural endings when the preceding phoneme is also _____. *(voiced, voiceless)*
whose x	15. The key symbol *z* represents the sound heard at the beginning of *zoo*. We noted above it is often represented by the grapheme *s*, as in _____ *(whose, quartz)* and also by the _____ as in *xylophone*.
s, azure	16. When we see the letter *z*, we expect it to represent the sound we hear at the beginning of *zoo*. The *z* occasionally stands for the sound represented by the key symbol _____ as in *quartz* and the key symbol *zh* as in _____. *(seize, azure)*

z z s s z s z	17. We have noted that several different graphemes may represent the initial sound heard in *sat* as well as the initial sound heard in *zoo*. To illustrate, write the key symbol which indicates the pronunciation of each of the underlined graphemes in the words at the right.

anxiety _____
is _____
its _____
scent _____
zone _____
circle _____
xylophone _____

sugar pleasure hose	18. We have also noted that the grapheme *s* may represent sounds other than that heard in *sat,* and that the grapheme *z* occasionally represents sounds other than that heard in *zoo*. Check the words at the right in which the *s* stands for a phoneme other than that heard at the beginning of *sat*.

sugar _____
this _____
pleasure _____
whisp _____
hose _____

waltz *azure*	19. Check the words at the right in which the *z* stands for a phoneme other than that heard at the beginning of the word *zoo*. *Zerox* _____ *waltz* _____ *azure* _____
voiceless	*f (far)* *v (van)* 20. Say the word *far*. Now start to say the word *far* again but hold the first sound. This is the sound we will represent by the key symbol *f*. The sound originates in the mouth, not in the vocal cords; it is a _____ sound. (voiced, voiceless)
voiced, *v*	21. Now hold the sound represented by the key symbol *f* while you note the position of your mouth. Add voice to the sound while you continue to hold the same position. You now have the counterpart of the sound represented by *f*. It is the _____ sound we represent by the key symbol _____. (voiced, voiceless)
voiced *f*	22. The *v* is a very reliable letter. That is, when we see the letter *v* in a word, we can be sure that it represents the sound we hear at the beginning of *van*. This is the _____ counterpart of the sound represented by the (voiced, voiceless) letter _____.
phoneme (or sound)	23. We can say, in regard to the *v*, there is a one-to-one correspondence between symbol and _____.
f *f* *f* *f* *v* *f*	24. The *f* is, in general, a reliable letter. Write the key symbol for the sound represented by *f* in each of the words at the right. *fine* _____ *fish* _____ *effect* _____ *off* _____ *of* _____ *if* _____
silent *off*	25. One *f* in the word *effect* is not sounded. It is clear then that *f* can be a _____ letter. Another example of an unsounded *f* in the previous frame is in the word _____.

v	26. The *f* represents the sound we associate with the key symbol _____ in the word *of.* (Try to pronounce *of* using the sound represented by the key symbol *f.*)
	27. We do not often use the letter *f* to represent the phoneme we associate with the key symbol *v.* But there are cases in which it would seem right to do so. It would be natural to spell the plural of *leaf* as *leafs,* but that is not the way we do it.
leaves	The plural of *leaf* is _____. We use the sound represented by the
v	key symbol _____ when we pronounce the plural of *leaf,* so we spell the word to conform. (Note that we do not follow this practice with regard to
z	the *s.* In the word *leaves,* we write *s* but say the sound represented by _____.)
f	28. What key symbol represents the sound of the under- *half* _____
v	lined letter in the words at the right? *halves* _____
f	*calf* _____
v	*calves* _____
	29. We have said that *f* is, in general, a reliable letter: when we see the letter *f* in a word, we expect, when the word is spoken, to hear the sound repre-
f	sented by the key symbol _____. On the other hand, there are other letters which are used to stand for the sound represented by the key symbol *f.* What
gh	letters represent the sound of *f* in the word *enough?* _____ In the word
ph	*phonics?* _____
	30. We have distinguished between voiceless and voiced phonemes illustrated
z, v	by two pairs of graphemes: the *s* and _____; the *f* and _____.
	Most of the consonant phonemes can be paired in like manner and will be presented in this part of the text in pairs. However, in only a few cases does that relationship add to the teacher's understanding of phonics for the teaching of reading. So further reference to voiced and voiceless phonemes will be limited to those cases where these properties are important in teaching reading.

REVIEW 2

1. The key symbol which represents the initial sound heard in *city* and the final sound heard in *quartz* is

_____.

2. The key symbol which represents the initial sound heard in *zero* and the final sound heard in *dogs* is

_____.

3. Generalizations:

   a. Consonant letters may represent more than one sound.

   The *s* represents the sound of _____ (as the key symbol indicates), of _____ *(sure)*, of _____ *(has)*, and of _____ *(treasure)*.

   The *z* represents the sound of _____ (as the key symbol indicates), of _____ *(quartz)*, and of _____ *(azure)*.

   b. Consonant sounds may be represented by more than one letter.

   The sound we hear at the beginning of *say* is often represented by *s*, by _____ *(cent)*, by _____ *(scene)*, and by many other graphemes.

   The sound we hear at the beginning of the word *zoo* is sometimes represented by the letters _____ and _____.

4. Reread the generalizations above (3a and b). Be sure you determine the difference between the two. These generalizations would carry more precise meanings if the words phoneme and grapheme were used. Then they would read:

   a. Consonant _____ may represent more than one _____.

   b. Consonant _____ may be represented by more than one _____.

5. Fill in the blanks. For . . ., use words from the right.

   a. The letter *v* is very reliable; we know that it always has the sound heard at the beginning of the word. . . . .

   b. When making plurals of some words ending in *f*, we change the sound to that represented by _____, and we also change the spelling from *f* to _____.
   Example: . . . . (singular); _____ (plural)

   c. The letter *f* is quite reliable. However, it may be silent, as in the word. . . . . .

   d. *f* represents the sound of *v* in the word. . . . .

   e. Other symbols are also used to represent the sound of *f*, as _____ in *cough* and _____ in *graph*.

   if
   of
   wolf
   far
   van
   sat
   zoo
   buff
   love

6. Rewrite the following words using the key symbols for the sounds represented by the under-lined letters:

   enough _____   *huff* _____   *zones* _____

   belief _____   *beliefs* _____   *falls* _____

   very _____   *believes* _____

   of _____   *books* _____

(See the Appendix for the answers to Review 2)

p/b, t/d

	p (pan) *b (bat)*
	1. We have thus far identified 4 of the 25 consonant phonemes. These phonemes have been easy to say in isolation. However, most consonant phonemes cannot easily be pronounced without adding a bit of a vowel sound. Some teachers, trying to pronounce the initial phoneme in *pan* say *puh.* To teach a child to say *puh* will not help him or her to identify the word *pan: puh—an* is not *pan!* Some experts advise teachers to say, "the first sound we hear in *pan*" or "the last sound we hear in *jump*" rather than attempt to sound the phoneme in isolation.
consonant	Keep in mind that it is very difficult to sound most _____ phonemes in isolation. (consonant, vowel)
p, grasp	2. In this study, we are establishing a key symbol for each phoneme in our language. The logical key symbol to use to identify the first phoneme heard in *pan* is _____. It is the last phoneme heard in _____. *(grasp, graph)*
p	3. We establish a key symbol and a key word to help distinguish this phoneme from any other. *Pan* is the key word we have selected to identify the sound represented by _____.
p	4. Next we examine its dependability. *P,* as a single consonant, is very reliable. When we see *p*, we can expect to hear the sound we are associating with the key symbol _____.
No *f*	5. Do we expect to hear the sound we associate with the key symbol *p* in *physics?* _____. The two-letter grapheme *ph* represents the sound we associate with the key symbol _____.
b *b*	6. Now let's turn our attention to the mate of *p,* the *b.* The logical key symbol to use to identify the first phoneme heard in *bat* is _____. The *b* is also very reliable. When we see the letter _____ we can expect it to represent the sound heard in the key word *bat.*

silent *bom* *driped, bobin*	7. Sometimes, however, the *p* and *b* have no phonemes: they are _____ (as in *happ/y, tom/b*). Rewrite these words, omitting the letters which represent no phonemes: *bomb* _____ *dripped* _____ *bobbin* _____ (Don't be concerned with the vowel sounds at this point. We'll indicate the vowel sounds later.)

senterz, above, bump *fobia, penz, prevent* *rober, flaper, sucses*	8. Rewrite the following words. Use the key symbols to indicate the sounds represented by the underlined letters. *cen ters* _____ *above* _____ *bump* _____ *phobia* _____ *pens* _____ *prevent* _____ *robber* _____ *flapper* _____ *success* _____

	t (tan) *d (doll)* 9. We shall represent the initial phoneme heard in *tan* and the initial phoneme heard in *doll* with the key symbols *t* and *d*, respectively. Say *tan* and *doll* aloud. Then listen carefully as you say the initial phonemes in *tan* and *doll*.
No	Are these phonemes easy to pronounce as isolated sounds? _____

t *d*	10. These letters are fairly dependable. The _____ may be silent as in *better,* and the _____ as in *lad/d/er.*

t	11. But let's examine more closely the sounds the *d* represents. The key symbol represents the sounds heard in *doll, did, do, led.* Now read these words out loud to discover another sound which the *d* represents: *puffed, clipped, hoped, missed* These *d's* represent the sound we associate with the key symbol _____. (Here again we note a relationship between the voiceless and voiced pair!)

hopt *puft* *slipt* one	12. Study each word at the right. *m issed* ___*mist*___ *Missed,* for example, has four phonemes. *hoped* _____ Rewrite each word showing the pronuncia- tion of the consonants by using key symbols. *puffed* _____ *slipped* _____ In spite of their appearance, these are all _____-syllable words. <div align="center">(one, two)</div>

t, one d	13. We have noted that the *d* sometimes is pronounced as though it were _____ (as in *kissed*). Now examine the words below. They are also _____ -syllable words. The final consonant represents the sound we associate with the key symbol _____. screamed served called (When the suffix *ed* does not form a separate syllable, we are inclined to use the voiceless *t* following a voiceless consonant and the voiced *d* following a voiced consonant.)
two ed d t, d	14. Notice the sound the *d* represents when *ed* forms a separate syllable. Say each of these words out loud. These are _____ -syllable words. In each the suffix _____ forms a separate syllable. The final *d* represents the sound assigned to the key symbol _____. Look at the letters preceding the suffixes (*seated*). They are either _____ or _____. *seated* *wanted* *waited* *needed* *sanded* *folded*
syllable d d	15. In general, the suffix *ed* forms a separate _____ when it is preceded by *t* or _____. When the *ed* forms a separate syllable, the final *d* represents the sound we associate with the key symbol _____.
d t	16. To summarize: When the suffix *ed* forms a separate syllable, the *d* represents the sound associated with the key symbol _____. When the suffix does not form a separate syllable, the *d* may represent the sound associated with the key symbol *d* or with the key symbol _____.
t th	17. We have noted that the *d* and *t* are fairly dependable. When we see a _____, we expect it to represent the sound of the first phoneme we hear in *tan*. Examine these words: <u>th</u>is, <u>th</u>en, wi<u>th</u>. We do not hear the sound represented by *t* in the two-letter grapheme _____. We will study this grapheme later.

REVIEW 3

1. Are the *p* and *b* reliable; that is, when we see one in a word, can we be quite sure of the sound it represents? _____

2. Rewrite the nonsense words at the right. Use the proper key symbol to indicate the sound the underlined letter would be most likely to represent.

phabap   _____

zaabs   _____

baps   _____

3. The *s* following the voiced consonant above is most likely to represent the sound we associate with the key symbol _____, which is the voiced counterpart of the *s*. This is illustrated by the nonsense word _____.

   (zaabs, baps)

4. Although *d* and *t* may be _____ (as in *letter* and *ladder*), they are generally quite reliable in the sound each represents.

5. The most common exception is in the case of the suffix _____.

6. Indicate, by using the key symbol, the sound we can expect the *d* to represent when the suffix forms a syllable of its own. _____

7. Indicate, by using key symbols, the sounds we can expect the *d* to represent in each of the following nonsense words:

lupped _____   *lubbed* _____   *luffed* _____   *luved* _____

(See the Appendix for the answers to Review 3.)

ch/j, k/g

	ch (chair) *j (jam)* 1. Say the word *jam* out loud. Now pronounce the first phoneme in that word. We will represent the initial sound heard in *jam* with the key symbol *j*. Its counterpart, the initial sound heard in *chair,* will be represented by the key symbol *ch*.
no	Is this the same phoneme as the initial sound heard in *city*? _____
two	2. Earlier, we learned that we would divide the 25 consonant phonemes into two categories: 18 of them would be represented by one-letter symbols and 7 by _____-letter symbols.
ch	3. We have no single letter in the alphabet to represent the first phoneme we hear in *chair*. We use the logical two-letter combination, the _____, to identify this phoneme. (Some systems use *č*.)
digraph	4. We call these two-letter combinations digraphs. Note the spelling—di for two; graph referring to writing. The two-letter combination *ch* as in *chair* is called a _____.

not	5. Pronounce the word *chair* as though <u>each</u> consonant were sounded. You said either *"s-hair"* or *"k-hair."* Now pronounce *chair* as it should be pronounced. Note that you hear neither the sound represented by the *c* nor by the *h*. The combination *ch* represents a phoneme _____ represented by (already, not) a single consonant letter. It functions like another letter of the alphabet.
digraph *c* *h*	6. A _____ is a two-letter combination which represents a single speech sound. The digraph *ch* does not represent the sound of the _____ and the _____ with which it is spelled.

no	7. Study the digraphs in these sets of words:
	
	        1 2 3
	  chair *character* *chiffon*
	  chalk *chord* *machine*
	  churn *chaos* *chute*
	
	Each word contains the grapheme *ch*. Does each grapheme represent the phoneme we associate with the key symbol *ch*? _____ Try pronouncing each one using the first phoneme in *chair* for each digraph.

ch *k* If you guessed *sh*, you are right!	8. The digraph in each of the words in set 1 of frame 7 represents the phoneme we associate with the key symbol _____. The digraphs in set 2 represent the phoneme we associate with the key symbol _____. Can you guess what key symbol represents the digraphs in set 3? _____
no *ch, k, sh*	9. Is the digraph *ch* reliable as to the phoneme it represents? _____ If we do not know the word, we cannot tell which key symbol to identify with it. It might be _____, or _____, or _____. (However, if you are an expert on language derivation, you will have clues.)
mach *queschon* *each*	10. The phoneme represented by the key symbol *ch* is not always spelled with a *c* and an *h*. Examine these words <u>carefully</u>. If the underlined part is the same as the first phoneme in *chair,* rewrite it using the key symbol. *ma*tch _____ *a*che _____ *quest*ion _____ *ea*ch _____ s*ch*ool _____

j	11. The voiced mate to the first sound heard in *chair* is the phoneme represented by the key symbol _____ and heard in *jam*.
gem *edge* *soldier*	12. Each of these words is written with the underlined part as it would appear in a pronunciation guide. How is each word spelled? *jem* _____ *ej* _____ *soljer* _____
j, g, dg, di	13. You will recall that the key symbol identifies a specific sound. What graphemes represent the sound we associate with the key symbol *j* in these words: *joke* _____ *gem* _____ *edge* _____ *soldier* _____
page	14. The initial sound heard in the word *jam* is often represented by the letter *g* as in _____. (*gift, page*)
j *j* *g*	15. *g* is the key symbol for the hard sound we hear at the beginning of *go.* We have noted that the letter *g* often represents the <u>soft</u> sound we associate with the key symbol _____. Are these used interchangeably or is there a pattern to the words which might give a clue as to whether the *g* represents the soft sound we associate with the key symbol _____ or the hard sound we identify with the key symbol _____? Let us examine some known words to see.
1. *gate* 2. *gem* 3. *giant* 4. *gone* 5. *gush* 6. *gym*	16. Study the sets of words below. Add a word from the list at the right to each set. Choose a word in which the *g* represents the same phoneme as the other underlined letters in the set and has the same vowel following the underlined *g*. *gone* *gem* *gush* *get* *gym* *gate* *giant*
e, i, y	17. The letter *g* usually represents the sound we associate with the key symbol *j* (the soft sound) when it is followed by the vowels _____, _____, or _____. (Carefully study the sets of words above before you answer.)

For item 16:

1	2	3	4	5	6
gain	*gentle*	*giraffe*	*go*	*gun*	*gypsy*
against	*age*	*engine*	*rigor*	*regular*	*geology*
_____	_____	_____	_____	_____	_____

get	18. The word "usually" in the generalization indicates that this is not always true.
	The word _____ is an exception. When *g* is followed by the letter
	(gem, get)
j	*e,* the *g* usually represents the sound we associate with the key symbol _____.
get	The word _____ does not follow this generalization.
	(get, gentle)
	19. Make a generalization about the phoneme that we associate with the key symbol *g*: The letter *g* usually represents the sound we associate with the
a, o, u	key symbol *g* when it is followed by the vowels _____, _____, or _____.
	20. What happens when other letters follow *g*? Study the words at the right.
	great
	ghost
	telegram
	The generalization will read: The *g* usually represents the soft
e, i, y	sound when followed by _____, _____, or _____. When followed *gleam*
hard (or the one	by any other letter or when it appears at the end of a word, the *egg*
associated with *g*)	*g* represents the _____ sound.
	Remember these sets: *j-eiy g-aou*
	21. Don't forget that there are exceptions. The generalization above, however, is a useful one. When you see a word you do not recognize, a word which contains a *g*, try the generalization.
e, i, y	Try the phoneme represented by the key symbol *j* when the *g* is followed by
	_____, _____, or _____; otherwise, try the hard sound, represented by the
g	key symbol _____.
	k *(kid)* g *(go)*
	22. We have noted that *g* has been selected as the key symbol to represent
hard	the _____ phoneme heard at the beginning of the word *go*. It is
	(hard, soft)
gull	the initial sound heard in _____.
	(gentle, gull)
silent	23. *G* is not a reliable grapheme. For example, it may be _____
j	as in *gnat.* It may represent the sound we associate with _____ as in *giant.*

a, o, u	24. With exceptions, there are some patterns of behavior. We have already learned that *g* generally represents the sound of its key symbol when it is followed by _____, _____, or _____.
g	25. The key symbol for a single consonant *g* at the end of a word is usually _____. *(g, j)*
hard kill	26. Now pronounce the word *kid.* Listen to the initial phoneme in *kid.* We will use the key symbol *k* to represent this hard sound. Listen for this phoneme in *back.* We use the key symbol *k* to represent the _____ sound heard at (hard, soft) the beginning of the word _____. *(kill, knight)*
canary, queen school, antique, lack	27. The phoneme associated with the key symbol *k* is represented by several different graphemes. Study the words below. Circle those in which the underlined letters represent the sound we associate with the key symbol *k:* canary cent queen school antique lack church
c, q, ch, ck	28. What graphemes represent the phoneme we associate with the key symbol *k* in the words in the frame above? _____ _____ _____ _____.
k, silent	29. The grapheme *ck* represents the phoneme we identify by the key symbol _____. Or we can say that the *c* (in the grapheme *ck*) is _____ (that is, not sounded).
better, ladder, happy, buff	30. Study these words: *better, ladder, happy, buff.* Put a slash through the silent letter in each. (We consider the second of the pair of like consonants to be silent.) Instead of following the "double consonant pattern" for *k*, we use the pattern *ck* (*duck, lacking,* etc.).
ck, c	31. In *duck* and *lacking,* the phoneme heard at the beginning of *kid* is represented by _____ (although we would be just as correct to say that the _____ in *lacking* is silent).

Consonants   29

k	**32.** The *q* <u>always</u> represents the sound we associate with the key symbol _____ .
	Rewrite these words using key symbols for the sounds represented by the underlined graphemes:
applikue, unikue, kuik	appli<u>q</u>ue _____ uni<u>q</u>ue _____ <u>q</u>uick _____
	(Of course, we are not indicating the true pronunciation because we are not considering the *u (w)*, silent letters, and vowels at this time.)

nob	**33.** Study the words at the right. Say them out loud. *knob* _____
unnon	*unknown* _____
nit	The *k* is silent at the beginning of a word *knit* _____
n *nak*	or syllable when followed by _____ . *knack* _____
	Rewrite these words; omit all letters which are silent. There are many words which follow this pattern.

n	**34.** Although *k* is silent when followed by the letter _____ , *k* can be considered quite a reliable letter. Let us be sure we understand: There are other graphemes which represent the sound we associate with the key symbol *k*, but when we see the letter *k* in a word, we can be quite sure that when we
phoneme	hear the word, we will hear the same _____ as that heard at the beginning of *kid.*

	35. We have noted that the phoneme whose key symbol is *k* is represented by
q, ch	different graphemes (as _____ in *queen* and _____ in *school*). One grapheme
cow	which deserves more study is the *c* as in _____ .
	(cow, cell)

c	**36.** Study these words: *cute, city.* Both start with the letter _____ . The first phoneme in *cute* represents the sound we associate with the key symbol
k	_____ . The first phoneme in *city* represents the sound we associate with the
s	key symbol _____ .

k	**37.** As a single-letter grapheme, the *c* not only represents no phoneme of its own, but commonly serves to represent <u>two</u> other phonemes, the _____ and
s	the _____ .
	There are some clues to guide us to the sounds the *c* represents in words we do not know.

38. Study the sets of words below. Add a word from the list at the right to each set.

coat
encyclopedia
city
curl
cent
cat

For each set below, choose a word from the six at the right in which the *c* represents the same phoneme as the other underlined letters in the set and has the same vowel following it.

1	2	3	4	5	6
cane	*cell*	*circus*	*comic*	*cue*	*cymbal*
decay	*mice*	*recite*	*recover*	*circus*	*bicycle*

———— ———— ———— ———— ———— ————

Check to see if you followed the directions.

1. *cat* 2. *cent* 3. *city*
4. *coat* 5. *curl*
6. *encyclopedia*

1, 4, 5

a, o, u

39. Which sets of words in frame 38 have *c*'s which represent the hard sound, that of the *k*? _____

What vowels follow the *c* in each of the these groups? _____

---

a, o, u

40. Complete the generalization: The letter *c* usually represents the sound we associate with the *k* when it is followed by _____, _____, or _____.

---

s, e, i, y

41. What about the "soft" sound? The letter *c* usually represents the sound we associate with the _____ when it is followed by _____, _____, or _____.

The letter *g* usually represents the soft sound *(j)* when it is followed by *e, i,* or *y.*

42. What is the generalization about the phoneme we associate with the soft sound of *g*?

---

yes

a, o, u
e, i, y

43. Are there similarities between the generalizations concerning the sounds represented by *c* and *g*? _____ The combined generalization might read: The consonants *c* and *g* represent their hard sounds when followed by _____, _____, and _____. They usually represent their soft sounds when followed by _____, _____, and _____.

k, g hard hard	44. Study the words at the right. What happens when other letters follow *c* and *g*? The *c* then represents the sound we associate with _____ and the *g* the sound we associate with _____. These are the _____ sounds. What happens when *c* or *g* is the last letter in the word? In that position they also represent their _____ sounds.

regret
gleam
crazy
comic
climb
big

e, i, y hard	45. Let's summarize the generalizations: The *c* and the *g* usually represent their soft sounds when followed by _____, _____, or _____. When followed by any other letter or when they appear at the end of the word, the *c* and the *g* represent their _____ sounds.

cello (pronounced *chello*) *girl* *giddy* *give*	46. Now apply the generalizations to the words at the right. Place a check mark next to the words which <u>do not</u> follow the generalization.

cube	*giant*
cello	*girl*
cotton	*guide*
cash	*giddy*
receive	*give*

REVIEW 4

1. Rewrite the following words, using the key symbol to show the pronunciation of each of the underlined graphemes (omit silent consonants):

   chara<u>c</u>ter _____   s<u>ch</u>ools _____   e<u>gg</u>s _____   <u>c</u>oat _____

   la<u>ck</u> _____   <u>gh</u>osts _____   anti<u>qu</u>e _____   <u>c</u>eiling _____

2. Write the key symbol which indicates the pronunciation of the last phoneme in each of the following words:

   beg _____   church _____   judge _____   quack _____

   knowledge _____   back _____   ache _____   unique _____

3. Write the key symbol which indicates the pronunciation of the first phoneme in each of the following words:

   Christmas _____   church _____   judge _____   quack _____

   ghastly _____   giraffe _____   knee _____   century _____

4. The key symbol _____ usually indicates the sound represented by the grapheme *c* when followed by *e*, _____, or *y*.

5. We can expect the key symbol _____ to indicate the sound represented by the grapheme *g* when followed by *a*, _____, or *u*.

6. When the grapheme *g* is not followed by a vowel, we expect the *g* to represent the sound of the key symbol _____.

7. Are the above generalizations always to be counted on? _____

(See the Appendix for the answers to Review 4)

wh/w, sh/zh, th/t̶h̶

w	*wh (why)* *w (we)* 1. Say *we* out loud. Listen to the first phoneme as you say *we*. The initial sound heard in *we* will be identified by the key symbol _____.
went, always	2. Use the words at the right for this and the following 5 frames to illustrate the characteristics of the consonant *w*. The consonant grapheme *w* never appears at the end of a syllable. *W* is generally an initial consonant in a word or syllable as in _____ and in (select a two-syllable word) _____ and is followed by a vowel.
dwarf (*quilt* and *queen* are OK, too!)	3. The phoneme represented by *w* may, however, be part of a blend of two consonants as in _____.
quilt, queen	4. The grapheme *u*, when following *q*, often represents the consonant phoneme we associate with the key symbol *w*. We hear this when we say the words _____ and _____.
write	5. It is silent before *r* as in _____.
who (hoo)	6. Occasionally the letter *w* fools us. It appears to be a part of the digraph *wh* but is actually silent, as in _____. (This is a puzzle. Can you solve it?)
one *once*	7. We are familiar with the word *won*. But notice the grapheme we use in the word pronounced the same but spelled _____. We use the same grapheme to represent the *w* in _____.

The words at the right of frame 2:

once
quilt
went
write
antique
who
dwarf
one
queen
always

Consonants   33

w silent	8. A review of the above will show that, although we use other graphemes to represent the *w*, it is a reliable letter. When we see a *w* we can expect it to represent the phoneme we associate with the key symbol _____. However sometimes it is _____ (as in *wrong*).
which	9. Now let's turn our attention to the counterpart of *w*, the phoneme we represent by the key symbol *wh* as heard at the beginning of the word _____. (Say these words out loud.) *(who, which)*
di (digraph) alphabet	10. *Wh* is a single phoneme, but the key symbol has two letters so we call it a _____ graph. We use *wh* as a key symbol because there is no letter in the _____ to represent this sound. We will use *why* as the key word to identify the phoneme.
w You are correct, whatever your response.	11. This phoneme may give you some trouble because it is rapidly disappearing from our language. If you pronounce *weather* and *whether* exactly the same, you are following the trend in America. Many people make the phoneme represented by the key symbol *wh* sound like that represented by its counterpart, the _____. What do you do? Pronounce *whistle, white*. Do they sound like *wistle, wite*? _____
wh *while*	12. Most dictionaries note this trend but continue to indicate the pronunciation of words beginning with *wh* as *hw*. We will use the key symbol _____ to represent the sound of the digraph, although it actually is better represented by *hw*. *Wh* represents the phoneme heard in _____. (Pronounce *whom* *(whom, while)* and *while* carefully so that you will hear the distinction.)
beginning	13. The *wh* digraph is found at the _____ of a word or syllable, *(beginning, end)* as is the *w*.
digraph beginning	14. The *w* and the d_____ *wh* are alike in that they are both reliable as to the sound(s) they represent. Both appear at the _____ of the word or syllable and are followed by a vowel.

sh (ship)   zh (pleasure)

15. The sound heard at the beginning of ship is very common, but there is no letter in the alphabet to represent it.

We shall use the key symbol *sh* to represent the phoneme as heard in the key

ship

word _____.

       (ship, clip)

---

one

16. When *s* and *h* appear together in this order in a syllable, we expect them

to represent _____ phoneme(s). Can you hear the separate

      (How many?)

no

phonemes represented by *s* and *h* in *shut?* _____ If you could, you'd hear the word *hut* in *shut.*

---

digraph

17. *Sh* is called a _____ because it represents one phoneme but is composed of two letters.

---

18. The phoneme we represent by *sh* has a variety of graphemes; that is, it is spelled in a variety of ways. Examine the words below. Look at the underlined parts. Rewrite the words using *sh* to represent the underlined graphemes.

shure, ship, moshon,   *sure* _____   *ship* _____   *motion* _____

shugar, mashine, speshal   *sugar* _____   *machine* _____   *special* _____

---

19. The graphemes which we associate with the key symbol *sh* are:

s, sh, ti   _____ in *sure*   _____ in *ship*   _____ in *motion*

s, ch, ci   _____ in *sugar*   _____ in *machine*   _____ in *special*

---

no

20. Now listen for the middle consonant sound as you say *pleasure.* Is there a letter in the alphabet to represent this sound? _____

---

zh

21. We shall use the digraph *zh* as the key symbol to represent the phoneme heard in *pleasure,* although it is never represented in a word with the grapheme _____.

---

pleazhure

vizhon

sabotazhe

azhure

pich

22. Rewrite the words at the right to indicate, by using the key symbols, the sounds of the underlined letters.

pleasure _____

vision _____

sabotage _____

azure _____

pitch _____

s, g	23. What letter represents the sound we associate with *zh* in *measure?* _____ In *rouge?* _____
sh ship	24. We can call *sh* reliable in that, when we see *sh* in a word, we can be quite sure it represents the sound we associate with the key symbol _____ as it is heard in the key word _____.
never	25. *Zh* _____ appears in a word, so it is not appropriate to make (never, seldom) a similar statement regarding reliability.

th (thin)   t̶h̶ (that)

26. Listen for the first phoneme while you pronounce *that* aloud. Compare it with the first phoneme in *thin.* Now we must recall what we learned about voiced and voiceless phonemes.

that

The voiced phoneme is represented by the *th* in _____; the voice-
                                                        (that, thin)

thin

less phoneme by the *th* in _____.
                          (that, thin)

27. You <u>must</u> say these words aloud or you will not hear the voiced quality. Note that the voiceless phoneme has a whispered sound even when you say it aloud.

thistle

The *th* in _____ has a whispered or voiceless sound. Our vocal
              (this, thistle)
cords do not vibrate.

28. Many people do not realize that *th* is a grapheme which represents two sounds just as different as the sounds represented by *p*

z

and *b* or *s* and _____.

thumb	They automatically use the correct sound for the words they have heard before. Check the words at the right in which the *th* represents the voiceless phoneme. You will not be able to tell the difference if you do not say them out loud!

thumb
the
though

thought

thought
them
they

thank
through
length
both

thank
through
length
both

together, think, throw	29. Repeat all the words in the previous frame in which the *th* represents the voiceless phoneme. Then say all the words in which the *th* represents the voiced phoneme. We shall use *th* as the key symbol to represent the voiced sound. We shall use *th* as the key symbol to represent the voiceless sound. Rewrite the following words; underline the digraphs which represent the voiceless phonemes and put a slash through the digraphs which represent the voiced phoneme. together _____ think _____ throw _____
phoneme voiced, *their*	30. When we see an unknown word in our reading containing the digraph *th,* we have no way of knowing which _____ it represents. We can use the dictionary. Many dictionaries use the slash to indicate that the *th* represents the v_____ phoneme as in _____. *(their, worth)*
the, bath	31. The *th* is not a reliable digraph. It may represent the voiced sound heard in _____ or the voiceless sound heard in _____. *(the, thief)* *(bath, bathe)*

REVIEW 5

Check yourself: Are you writing every answer and finishing each frame before moving the mask down? Are you getting almost every answer correct? Do you study more carefully when you miss one? Do you analyze your errors? Can you give yourself 100 on each review?

1. A grapheme composed of two letters which represent a single sound is called a _____.

2. Indicate the pronunciation of the underlined parts of the following words by using key symbols:

quick _____	who _____	measure _____	whether _____
which _____	both _____	weather _____	notion _____
sugar _____	wish _____	vision _____	wrong _____
those _____	of _____	thrive _____	know _____

3. Underline all the consonant digraphs in the following words which serve as key symbols and cannot be replaced by a single letter from our alphabet:

weather	enough	whom	which
wrist	wish	both	through

(See the Appendix for the answers to Review 5)

m, n, ng

	m (man) n (not) ng (sing)
	1. Say *man, not, sing.* Then pronounce the first phoneme in *man* and *not* and the last phoneme in *sing.* These are all voiced phonemes. Hold your nose while you repeat these three phonemes aloud. That was asking the impossible! You can see why they are called nasal sounds.
one	You will note that the *ng* represents _____ phoneme(s).
	(How many?)
digraph	Since this grapheme has two letters, it is called a _____.
nasal	2. The *m* is a very reliable letter. The other two phonemes in the group, classified as _____ sounds (because the air passes through the nose), need more study.
2	3. The *n* and *g* represent _____ phoneme(s) in *ungrateful.* The *n* and *g* repre-
	(How many?)
1	sent _____ phoneme(s) in *thing.*
think	4. Say *thing.* Add the phoneme represented by *k* to *thing (thing + k).* We do not spell this word *thingk:* we spell it _____. The phoneme we
n	identify with the key symbol *ng* is represented by the grapheme _____ in the word *think.*
tang + k	5. There are many words in which the phoneme we represent by *ng* is followed by *k* or *g.* Then the single letter *n* is used to represent the sound we associate with the key symbol *ng.*
	Pronounce *tank.* Which "key to pronunciation" at the right tan + k
	is correct? Check it. tang + k
fing ger	6. Pronounce the "words" at the right. This is hard! Which set of fin ger
	key symbols (consonant sounds only) indicates the correct pro- fin jer
	nunciation of *finger?* Check it. fing ger
	fing jer
ng, g	7. In *finger,* the *n* represents the sound we associate with the key symbol _____. The *g* represents the sound we associate with the key symbol _____. To show pronunciation, we need both the *ng* and the *g.*

kang ga roo kon grat u late	8. Which set of symbols below indicates the pronunciation of *kangaroo?* Of *congratulate?* *kan ga roo kan ja roo kang ga roo kang ja roo* *con grat u late kon grat u late cong grat u late kong grat u late*

ran
 	
bank (bangk)
	9. It is clear that the grapheme *n* sometimes represents the phoneme associated with the key symbol *n,* as in _____, and sometimes with the key
	                  (ran, rang)
	symbol *ng,* as in _____.
	         (bank, band)

conglomerate	10. We have also noted that when we see *n* and *g* together in a word, the *ng* may represent the two separate phonemes which we associate with the separate symbols *n* and *g* as in _____. *(conglomerate, clang)*
digraph gingham	11. The letters *n* and *g* together in a word are most commonly a _____, that is, a two-letter combination representing a single phoneme, as in _____. *(gingham, ungrateful)*
lingo	12. The letters *n* and *g* may also represent the sounds we associate with the key symbols *ng* and an additional *g,* as in _____. *(nongaseous, lingo)*
end	13. The *ng* digraph is always found at the _____ of a word or *(beginning, end)* syllable.
silent	14. The *n* is often _____ after *m,* as in *hymn, solemn.*
n ng	15. We use the key symbol _____ to represent the last phoneme heard in *pan.* We use the key symbol _____ to represent the last phoneme heard in *bring.* Some dictionaries use the phonetic symbol η to indicate the last phoneme in *bring.*

REVIEW 6

1. The phonemes represented by _____, _____, and _____ are called nasal sounds. They are all
   _____.
   (voiced, voiceless)

2. What grapheme represents the phoneme we identify by the key symbol *ng* (or η) in *sing?* _____

3. In *single?* _____ (Pronounce carefully. What part of *single* represents the sound we hear in *sing?*)

4. What grapheme represents the final phoneme in *condemn?* _____

5. What grapheme represents the final phoneme in *plan?* _____

6. The two-letter key symbols *ch* and *ng* are called _____.

7. Rewrite the following words; use key symbols to indicate the pronunciation of the underlined parts.
   Omit silent consonant letters. Underline the digraphs.

   range _____   *rankle* _____   *ransom* _____

   manger _____   *mangle* _____   *links* _____

8. As a single letter, we can expect *g* to represent the hard sound we associate with the key symbol *g,* except
   when followed by _____, _____, or _____.

9. When *g* is part of a _____ as in *enough,* it is not considered a single-letter consonant: The *g*
   in *enough* does not represent the sound we associate with the key symbol g as in _____.
   (go, ginger)

   The *g* in *enough* does not represent the sound we associate with the key symbol _____ as in *gem.*

   Nor is the *g* in *enough* a _____ letter as it is in *knight.*

(See the Appendix for the answers to Review 6.)

h, l, r, y

	h (he) l (let) r (run) y (yes)
	1. We will use the key symbol *h* to represent the voiceless consonant heard at the beginning of the word *he.*
final	This phoneme is never heard as the _____ sound of a word or (initial, final) syllable.
silent	2. The letter *h* is a dependable letter, except that it is very often _____ (as in *hour*).

oh, hurrah, hallelujah	3. *H* is silent when it follows the vowel in a word or syllable. Put a slash through the silent *h*'s in the following words: oh hurrah hallelujah Check carefully. Do you hear the phoneme represented by *h?*
heir, honor, honest	4. The *h* may even be silent when it appears as the initial consonant of a word. There are no clues to tell us whether or not the initial *h* represents a phoneme. In fact, some people consider the *h* to be silent in *homage, humble, herb.* Circle the words below in which the initial *h* is silent: here heir honor habit honest
g, k r	5. Study the words at the right. The letter *h* is silent when it follows the consonants _____, _____, and _____. ghost khaki rhyme ghastly khan rheumatism
voiced voiceless	6. The phoneme we represent by the key symbol *h* has no _____ (voiced, voiceless) counterpart. The voiced phonemes we represent by the grapheme *l* (as in *lot*), *r* (as in *run*) and *y* (as in *yes*) have no v_____ counterparts in the English language.
silent	7. As single consonant letters, the *l, r,* and *y* are reliable letters. When the *l* or the *r* appear as double letters *(tall, hurry)* the second of each set of like consonants is _____.
l m, k, d	8. The letter _____ is sometimes silent when followed in the same syllable by _____, _____, or _____. Examine the words at the right to determine this answer. calm yolk folk would
yellow, yet, yacht, beyond	9. The first phoneme heard in *yes* is a consonant represented by the key symbol *y*. This sound is heard only at the beginning of a word or syllable. Be sure you do not confuse it with the vowel phoneme. Which words have the phoneme represented by the key symbol *y* (consonant)? yellow yet play ice bicycle yacht beyond Now check yourself. Do they have the phoneme heard at the beginning of *yes?* Do they hold the initial position of the syllable?

REVIEW 7

1. We have identified each of the 7 graphemes which serve as additions to our alphabet. Six of them are contained in the words below. Write the key symbol following the word in which each is found.

   chording _____ *white* _____ *measure* _____ *there* _____ *photoflash* _____ *blanch* _____

2. One grapheme is missing from the group of digraphs above. It is found in _____.
   (breath, breathe)

3. We have identified all of the 18 single-letter phonemes. They are heard in the initial position in each of the following words: *bat, doll, far, go, he, jam, kid, lot, man, not, pan, run, sat, tan, van, we, yes, zoo.* Select key words from those above to illustrate phonemes represented by the underlined graphemes below. Those which have no key word may be left blank.

   Examples: *work* _we_ *psychology* _____

(1) could _____	(5) gist _____	(9) of _____	(13) my _____
(2) yonder _____	(6) bomb _____	(10) get _____	(14) wrong _____
(3) circle _____	(7) palm _____	(11) honor _____	(15) little _____
(4) jumped _____	(8) ghetto _____	(12) tall _____	(16) rag _____

4. The word *gem* _____ a key word because the *g* _____ represent the phoneme
               (is, is not)   (does, does not)
   we associate with the key symbol *g.*

5. The word *try* is not a key word for the *y* phoneme because the *y* is not at the beginning of the syllable; it is, therefore, not a _____ letter.
                     (consonant, vowel)

(See the Appendix for the answers to Review 7.)

Other Consonant Digraphs

	1. We have identified the 18 consonant phonemes which we represent with single-letter key symbols.
f, j, l, m, n, s	They are *b, d,* _____, *g, h,* _____, *k,* _____, _____, _____, *p, r,* _____,
t, z	_____, *v, w, y,* and _____.

digraphs	2. We have also identified the seven _____ which represent distinct phonemes not represented by the single letters in the alphabet. They are
church	(1) *ch* as in _____
	(church, choir)
sh	(2) _____ as in *wish*
zh	(3) _____ sounded like the *z* in *azure*
th	(4) _____ as in *think*
there	(5) *th* as in _____
	(there, thrill)
wheat	(6) *wh* as in _____
	(whole, wheat)
ng	(7) _____ as in *fling*

	3. We have identified the seven digraphs, each of which represents a distinct phoneme necessary to describe our language.
two	There are other digraphs; that is, other _____-letter combinations
	(How many?)
one	which represent _____ speech sound.
	(How many?)

	4. These digraphs are more commonly represented by other letters or other digraphs. What is the more common representation of each of the digraphs listed below?
f	*gh* as in *cough* _____
f	*ph* as in *phonics* _____
h	*wh* as in *who* _____

	5. Some two-letter combinations represent one sound and could be considered digraphs; however, this sound may be the sound represented by one of the letters. Let's take the word *who* (above) as an example. The *wh* could be called a *digraph,* or we could say that the *w* is silent—which leaves us with a phoneme represented by a single letter. What letters are silent in the following two-letter combinations:
c, p, w, w	*back* _____ *psychology* _____ *whole* _____ *whose* _____

	6. The *gh* combination can represent different sounds or no sound at all:
f	*enough* — Here *gh* is a digraph representing the phoneme we associate with the key symbol _____.
hard	*ghost* — The *gh* represents the _____ phoneme we associate
	(hard, soft)
g, h	— with the key symbol _____. The _____ is silent.
silent	*bough* — The *gh* is _____.
	slaughter

	7. Which of the following words contain consonant digraphs? Write the digraph following those words.
whopper wh	*whopper* _____ *myth* _____ *cream* _____
myth th	*blue* _____ *digraph* _____ *price* _____
digraph ph	

	8. Rewrite these words using appropriate key symbols for each consonant. Copy the vowels as they are.
kaos, thi, wich	*chaos* _____ *thigh* _____ *witch* _____
samz, fraze, lauf	*psalms* _____ *phrase* _____ *laugh* _____
(Congratulations!)	

REVIEW 8

1. There are 25 consonant sounds in the American-English language. We identify 18 of them with single-_____ symbols. We should have _____ more consonant letters in the alphabet. Since we don't, we use two-letter combinations called _____ to serve as key symbols for these phonemes. The two-letter symbols are:

2. Our sound-symbol system is complicated by the use of other consonant digraphs standing for phonemes already represented in the system. Select three examples of such digraphs from these words:

   tough, chalk, sheath, short-sighted, chloroform, phoneme

3. These three are already represented by (Use key symbols) _____, _____, _____.

4. Rewrite these words using the appropriate key symbols for the consonants. Copy the vowels as they are.

   thereof _____ *photograph* _____ *think* _____

   alphabet _____ *pheasant* _____ *cough* _____

(See the Appendix for the answers to Review 8.)

h, k, n, s, w	1. We have noted that there are 18 single-letter consonant phonemes and 7 consonant digraphs to represent the consonant sounds of our language.
	We have selected a key symbol to represent each of the 25 consonant phonemes. The key symbols representing the 18 single-letter phonemes are *b, d, f, g,* _____ *, j,* _____ *, l, m,* _____ *, p, r,* _____ *, t, v,* _____ *, y,* and *z.*
c q, x	2. Have you noticed that we omitted three consonant letters, the _____, _____, and _____?
k	3. These three single letters do not represent phonemes which have not already been represented. We have noted that the *q* always represents the phoneme which we associate with the key symbol _____. We do not use it as part of a digraph (as in the case of *c* in *ch*). In fact, we could do very well without it!
opak teknik k plak antik k, u, e	4. Study the words at the right. The *que* combination at the end of a word represents the phoneme we associate with the key symbol _____. Or we might say that the *q* represents the sound we associate with _____, while the _____ and _____ are silent. opaque _____ technique _____ plaque _____ antique _____ Rewrite these words using the proper key symbol to stand for each of the consonants. Omit the silent *"ue"* combination and the silent consonants.
u k	5. The letter *q* is almost always followed by the letter _____. In *opaque,* the *u* is silent. There are a few words which begin with *q* in which the *u* is also silent as in *quay,* or the *u* is pronounced as *u,* as in *queue.* We may miss this point because we may be mispronouncing these words. *Quay* is pronounced as though it were spelled *key; queue* is pronounced as though it were spelled *cue.* The first phoneme in both *key* and *cue* (therefore in *quay* and *queue*) is represented by the key symbol _____. Pronounce *quay* and *queue* correctly several times (*quay* as *key; queue* as *cue*).

k w	6. More commonly, the *u* following the letter *q* becomes a consonant and represents the sound we associate with the key symbol *w.* Say these words: *quit, equal, quiet, queen, quill.* In these words the *q* represents the sound we associate with _____ , and the *u* represents the sound we associate with _____ .
c k s	7. Study the words at the right. Both start with the letter _____ . The first phoneme in the first word represents the sound we associate with the key symbol _____ . The first phoneme in the second word represents the sound we associate with the key symbol _____ . *cart* *cent*
k, s	8. As a single-letter grapheme, the *c* represents no phoneme of its own. It could be replaced by the _____ and the _____ . There are clues to guide us to the sound the *c* represents in words we do not know.
a, o, u	9. Review the generalizations: The letter *c* usually represents the sound we associate with the *k* when it is followed by _____ , _____ , or _____ .
s e, i, y	10. The letter *c* usually represents the sound we associate with the _____ when it is followed by _____ , _____ , or _____ .
k	11. When followed by any other letter or when it appears at the end of a word, the *c* represents the sound we associate with the letter _____ .

fox (foks)
 	
Either is correct
	12. The letters *q* and *c* do not have key symbols to represent their sounds because they are already represented.
	
	The letter *x* is also an unnecessary letter. It represents the sounds we associate with the voiced combination *gz* or its voiceless counterparts *ks* (as in _____). And we often interchange them! How do you pronounce
	   (fox, exam)
	exit? _____
	   (egzit, eksit)

z eks	13. Then consider the word *xylophone.* At the beginning of a word, *x* consistently represents the sound we associate with the key symbol _____ . Of course, there are times when we use *x* as a letter: *X-ray* or *X-ograph.* In these instances, _____ could be used as the graphemes to represent the *x.*

gz, ks, z	14. The *x* could be omitted from our alphabet by using the letters (or combinations) _____, _____, _____. Spell the words at the right, substituting the proper graphemes for the letter *x* in each one.

	egzample	*example* _____
	boks	*box* _____
	zeroks	*Xerox* _____
	egzist	*exist* _____
	ekstreme	*extreme* _____
	zylem	*xylem* _____

k gz, ks, z ch, k s	15. The phonemes represented by *c, q,* and *x* need no key symbols. In our one-to-one correspondence, they are already represented. We could omit the letter *q* entirely by substituting the _____. We could omit the letter *x* by substituting _____, _____, or _____. We do use the *c* as part of the digraph _____, but as a single letter, the _____ and _____ could adequately take its place.

REVIEW 9

1. There are three consonants which, as single letters, represent no distinctive phonemes:

   a. The *c* usually represents the sound we associate with *s* when followed by _____, _____, or _____.
   The *c* usually represents the sound we associate with _____ when followed by the vowels _____, _____, or _____, most other consonants, or when appearing at the end of a word.

   b. The *q* always represents the sound we associate with _____.

   c. The *x* can adequately be represented by the consonants _____, _____, and _____.

2. There are other letters which represent two or more sounds, one of which is the sound we commonly associate with that particular letter (key symbol).

   a. The *g* represents "its own sound" (the _____ sound) when followed by the vowels _____, _____, _____, or by other consonants.

   (hard, soft)

   b. The *g* usually represents its _____ sound, that which we ordinarily associate with the

   (hard, soft)

   letter _____, when followed by _____, _____, _____.

3. The two most common sounds represented by the single letter *s* are:

    a. The sound we ordinarily associate with the letter *s,* as in _____ .

                                          (some, sugar)

    b. The sound we ordinarily associate with the letter _____ , as in *his.*

4. The letter *d* may represent the sound we associate with _____ or with _____ when it appears in the suffix *ed.*

5. *F* occasionally represents the sound we associate with _____ , as in *of.*

(See the Appendix for the answers to Review 9.)

Silent Letters

silent	1. As we examined the letters of the alphabet and the phonemes they represent, we noted that sometimes a letter represents no phoneme; that is, the letter is _____ .
k *khaki, g, ghost, r* *rhetoric* *hurrah,* beginning *hour*	2. Many generalizations can be made to help determine whether a letter represents a sound or no sound. We will not learn all the generalizations concerning these letters, but we should be able to recognize typical combinations. The following frames will call attention to certain patterns of silent letters. In most instances, this section will serve as a review. The letter *h* is silent when it follows the consonants _____ as in _____ , _____ as in _____ , or _____ as in _____ . *H* is silent when it follows a vowel as in _____ . Sometimes *h* is silent at the _____ of a word, as in _____ . *hurrah* *khaki* *hour* *ghost* *rhetoric*
silent *l, p*	3. When two like consonants appear together in a word, usually only the first represents a phoneme; the second is _____ . What letters are silent in the words at the right? _____ *tell* *supper*
k *s*	4. This generalization does not hold when the consonants represent different sounds. In the word *success,* the first *c* represents the sound we associate with the key symbol _____ , the second *c* the sound we associate with the key symbol _____ .

akses, stoping, bless, aksident, aksept	5. Examine the following words. Rewrite them using key symbols for the consonants. Omit the silent letters. access _____ stopping _____ bless _____ accident _____ accept _____
k n	6. Study these words: knave knead knee knickers knife know The _____ is silent at the beginning of a word when followed by the letter _____.
w r r, t	7. Note the words at the right. The _____ is generally silent when followed by _____ at the beginning of a word. What consonants are sounded in *wrought?* _____ *wrist* *wrinkle* *write* *wrench*
gh, t n, t	8. The _____ combination is usually silent when followed by _____. What consonants are sounded in *knight?* _____ *bright* *sight* *sought* *ought*
c n, k	9. In words containing *ck,* the _____ is usually silent. What consonants are sounded in *knock?* _____ *pluck* *dicker* *black* *back*
no s, t, n p	10. Is *p* sounded in the following words? _____ *pshaw psychology psalm ptomaine pneumatic pneumonia* When *p* is followed by _____, _____, or _____ at the beginning of a word, the _____ is usually silent.
l no (The *l* and *m* are not in the same syllable.)	11. The letter _____ is sometimes silent when followed by *m* or *k* in the same syllable. According to this generalization would you expect *l* to be silent in *helmet?* _____ *calm* *yolk* *folk*

m, t obtain	12. When *b* follows _____ or precedes _____ in the same syllable, the *b* is usually silent. What word does not belong in this group? _____	*climb* *comb* *limb* *doubt* *debt* *dumb* *obtain*

t, t often, soften, fasten listen, moisten	13. When _____ follows *f* or *s*, the _____ is sometimes silent. These words are written without the silent consonants; rewrite them correctly. ofen _____ sofen _____ fasen _____ lisen _____ moisen _____

silent sigh, through, knife	14. We should know that not all consonant letters represent phonemes. Some are _____. Which of these words have silent consonants? sigh through she knife piece your

REVIEW 10

1. There are 25 consonant sounds in the American-English language.
   a. We identify 18 of them with single-letter symbols. They are:

   b. We use _____ to identify the 7 additional phonemes. They are: _____

2. *C* was not included in 1.a. above because _____.

3. What other consonant letters were not included?

4. *Ph* was not included in 1.b. above because _____.

5. Rewrite the following words using appropriate key symbols for the consonants. Omit silent consonants.
   Copy vowels as they are.

wholesale _____	high _____	quick _____
pharynx _____	wholly _____	zephyr _____
thatch _____	psychic _____	taught _____
depot _____	glisten _____	daughter _____
rustle _____	doubt _____	knot _____
midget _____	wrap _____	supper _____

(See the Appendix for the answers to Review 10.)

Consonant Blends

1. We have identified each of the 25 consonant phonemes of the English language. Now let us turn our attention to some of the blends of these phonemes.

Examine the word *blue*. How many consonant phonemes does *blue* contain? _____ What are they? _____ _____

2, b, l

one

2. A digraph is a two-letter grapheme which represents _____ speech sound. The word *blue* does <u>not</u> contain a consonant digraph. Neither of the consonants, the _____ nor the _____, loses its identity. Both are sounded, but they are blended together. We call such combinations of consonant phonemes _____.

b, l

blends

We need to study the consonant blends, because in many ways they act as one phoneme.

3. A cluster of two or three consonants often represents a blend. Pronounce the words below. Note the sounds which the underlined consonants represent.

black	clown	flying	scream
break	chowder	fry	splinter

chowder (*Ch* is not a blend of the *c* and *h*.)

Which word does not belong in this list? _____

yes

Do you hear the consonant sounds you expect to hear when you pronounce the rest of these words? _____

4. Examine these sets of words. Each set has one of the common "blenders." Write the letter common to each consonant cluster in the set.

1	2	3
brown	flame	skate
great	claim	snow
strait	splinter	street

1. r, 2. l, 3. s

_____ _____ _____

r, l

s

5. The common blenders are represented by the letters _____, _____, and _____. However, there are blends which do not contain these letters.

blend digraph	6. We distinguish a _____ from a digraph by the fact that it repre-sents two or more phonemes blended together. The _____ repre-sents a single sound. Check those combinations in the following list which are not consonant blends.

<table>
<tr><td>sh</td><td>bl   cr   qu   sc   scr</td></tr>
<tr><td></td><td>cl   dr   tw   sh   spr</td></tr>
<tr><td>ch</td><td>gl   fr   ch   sm   spl</td></tr>
<tr><td>th</td><td>sl   pr   th   sw   str</td></tr>
</table>

w equal, quart, queen, quick	7. It may seem strange to classify *qu* as a consonant blend when *u* is a vowel. The *u* in this case, however, takes the sound of the consonant _____. So this combination is actually a *kw* blend. Select the words with the *kw* blend from the following: equal quart quay queen opaque quick
tr, tw, gr, spl, qu pl, str, sl, pr, fr (NOT ch or sh!)	8. Underline the consonant blends in these words: tree twin great splash chair quiet plow she street slow pretty free
s, h	9. The *sh* in *splash* and the *sh* in *she* cannot be blends because the sounds represented by the _____ and the _____ are not heard.
train, task	10. Consonant blends may appear at the beginning of a word or syllable, as in *train,* or at the end of a word or syllable, as in *task.* Underline the appropriate blend in both of these examples.

Blends Digraphs	11. Arrange the words below in two columns: those which contain blends and those which contain con-sonant digraphs. Some words may be used in both columns. Underline to indicate the part in each word which qualifies it to be in the particular column.	Blends Digraphs
trench trench rest church digraph digraph trash trash	trench, church, rest, digraph, trash	

th r through, shriek	12. Examine the word *thrush.* The first three letters contain a digraph _____ blended with the _____. There are many such words. Draw a single line under the digraph, and another line under the digraph-blend in these words: *through, shriek.*

Blends	Digraphs
toast	diphthong
grapheme	grapheme
thrush	thrush
clanging	clanging
strike	altogether
	father

13. Arrange the words below in two columns: those which contain blends and those which contain consonant digraphs. Some of these words, too, may be used in both columns, so underline to indicate the part of each word that places it in a column.

toast, diphthong, grapheme, thrush, clanging, strike, altogether, father

Blends	Digraphs

REVIEW 11

1. A blend differs from a digraph in that

2. Why were no key symbols given to represent the blends?

3. What blends appear in the following words: *The black engine can nudge the freight train off these tracks.*

4. What consonant digraphs appear in the words of the above sentence?

(See the Appendix for the answers to Review 11.)

III. Vowels

A reminder: Do not pull the mask down until you have responded to the entire frame.

vowels	1. The 26 letters of the alphabet are divided into two major categories: consonants and _____.
voiced	2. All vowel phonemes are produced by vibrating vocal cords. Vowel phonemes are, therefore, _____. (voiced, voiceless)
vowels	3. The letters *a, e, i, o, u,* and sometimes *w* and *y* are classified as _____.
yes	4. How can you tell when *y* is a consonant and when it is a vowel? You have learned that the key symbol *y* (consonant) represents the phoneme heard in _____. *Y* functions as a consonant <u>only</u> when it represents the (yes, say) phoneme heard in *yes.*
initial	5. The consonant *y* is always the _____ letter in a word or syllable. It is always found before the vowel. (initial, final)
consonant *yellow* *yet* vowel *beyond*	6. Study the words at the right. Underline each *y* which is a consonant. The _____ *y* is never a silent letter. The (consonant, vowel) _____ *y* is often a silent letter. (consonant, vowel) <div>they *yellow* *yet* may crazy *beyond*</div>

vowel	7. *Y* does not serve as a key symbol for a vowel phoneme. It represents no sound of its own. When *y* is a _____, its pronunciation is shown (consonant, vowel) by the key symbols we associate with the *i* or the *e*.
ꭨ^ceast nymph my lanyard ready lanyard	8. Study the function of the *y* in the words at the right. Place a <u>c</u> or a <u>v</u> above each *y* to identify *y* as a consonant or as a vowel. Check each *y* consonant to see that it represents the same sound as the initial phoneme in *yes*. In which word is the *y* the first letter in the second syllable? _____ *yeast* *nymph* *my* *ready* *lanyard*
we	9. Now let us examine the *w*. You have learned that *w* as a consonant represents the phoneme heard in _____. (we, two)
symbol	10. As a vowel, the *w* represents no distinct phoneme of its own. Therefore, it cannot be represented by a key _____. It is always used in combination with another vowel, as in *few, cow, two*.
t<u>wo</u>, thre<u>w</u> wh<u>ich</u>	11. Underline the *w*'s which function as vowels in the following words: *water, which, two, threw, dwarf*. (Be sure that they do not represent the phoneme you hear at the beginning of *we*.) The word _____ above contains a *w* which is a part of a consonant digraph.
w, y	12. Two of the seven vowels are not identified by distinctive key symbols because they do not represent sounds of their own. These are the vowels _____ and _____.
a, e i, o, u	13. Now let us turn our attention to the vowels which do represent phonemes and can be assigned key symbols to distinguish them from each other. The vowel phonemes are represented by five letters. They are _____, _____, _____, _____, _____.
cannot be	14. These five vowels, alone and in combination with another vowel, represent the 19 vowel phonemes of our language. Therefore, there _____ a (is, cannot be) one-to-one correspondence between phoneme and letter.

Vowels   55

a, 5	15. Study the words at the right. Pronounce the sound represented by the underlined vowel. s<u>a</u>me / d<u>a</u>re / c<u>a</u>n / <u>a</u>rm / <u>a</u>bout We can see that one vowel, the _____, represents at least _____ different phonemes.
phoneme vowels	16. Each vowel letter represents more than one _____. If we meet an unfamiliar word, how will we know which sounds its vowels represent? There are some patterns (with exceptions, of course) which will give us some help in determining the sounds represented by the _____ in un-known words.
phonemes vowel	17. Our task, then, is two-fold: (1) To identify the vowel _____ of the American-English language and assign each a key symbol. (2) To become acquainted with the generalizations which will aid us in associating the correct phonemes with the _____ letters in unknown words.
single digraphs	18. For our study, we shall divide the vowel phonemes into three major groups. (1) those represented by single letters (2) those represented by diphthongs } combinations of letters (3) those represented by digraphs Each of the _____ letters (as in group 1) and each of the com-binations of letters (whether diphthongs or _____) represent <u>one</u> phoneme.
letter	19. We shall begin our study of the vowel phonemes with Group 1: those represented by a single vowel _____. (letter, phoneme)

REVIEW 12

1. The vowel letters are _____, _____, _____, _____, _____, and sometimes _____ and _____.

2. We need not select key symbols to represent the sounds of _____ and _____, because they duplicate the sounds of other vowels.

3. Indicate whether the *w* and the *y* letters in these nonsense words are consonants or vowels by writing C or V following each word:

yagh _____   nylp _____   pnay _____   wehn _____   prew _____   whog _____

4. The *w* in *white* is part of a _____ _____.
   (consonant, vowel)

5. There are _____ vowel phonemes than there are vowel letters.
   (fewer, more)

(See the Appendix for the answers to Review 12.)

Long Vowel Sounds

	$\bar{a}$ *(lake)*　$\bar{e}$ *(me)*　$\bar{\imath}$ *(ice)*　$\bar{o}$ *(no)*　$\bar{u}$ *(use)*
name	1. One set of phonemes represented by single vowel letters are those which "say their own names." Pronounce the first word at the right. Make the sound represented by the underlined vowel; then say the name of the underlined vowel. *la͟ke* *m͟e* *i͟ce* *n͟o* *u͟se* The sound represented by the vowel is the same as the _____ of the vowel. Pronounce the rest of the words, vowel phonemes, and letter names the same way.
$\bar{e}$, $\bar{\imath}$, $\bar{o}$, $\bar{u}$	2. We indicate the pronunciation of the vowel letter which "says its own name" by placing a macron (¯) over it. Therefore the key symbol, as found in the dictionary, for the *a* in *lake* is $\bar{a}$. What would the key symbol be for each of the other underlined vowels in frame 1? _____ _____ _____ _____
pine	3. "Macron" contains the word element *macro*, which means "long" or "great." It has been the custom, in phonics, to call the vowel sound whose key symbol is a macron over the vowel letter, a "long vowel sound." Therefore, we would say the *i* in _____ represents a long vowel (pin, pine) sound.
long	4. It would seem that, in the normal pronunciation of words, we would hold long vowel sounds for a greater length of time than short vowel sounds. This is not necessarily true. Some texts now use the term "glided sound" rather than _____ to indicate the sound of a vowel that "says its own (long, short) name." We will use these terms interchangeably.

(If you had any incorrect, study them carefully. Does the *a* in *many* "say its own name"?) tāke, gō, fīne, bē, sāme	5. Place a macron above the vowels which represent long (glided) sounds in these words. Be sure the vowel "says its own name." take go many fine once all be same
cake, be, fine bone, accuse	6. These five vowel phonemes are represented by the key symbols ā, ē, ī, ō, ū. Select a word from the list at the right which illustrates each. ā _____ ē _____ ī _____ ō _____ ū _____ *be* *up* *cake* *accuse* *bone* *fine* *run*
tāmé, scēné, cūté bōné, Jōé, pīné	7. Study the words below. Indicate those vowels which represent their long (glided) sounds by placing macrons above them. Put a diagonal line (/) through each vowel which is silent. tame scene cute bone Joe pine
e e, long (glided)	8. There are many one-syllable words with two vowels in which *e* is the second vowel as well as the final letter of the word. We can make a generalization concerning these words. Study the words *tame* and *pine,* then complete this generalization: When a one-syllable word has two vowels, one of which is a final _____, the _____ is silent and the first vowel usually represents its _____ sound.
VCV	9. This generalization most often applies to words which have the ending pattern of VCV. The word *use* is an example of VCV: vowel, consonant, vowel. *Tame* and *plate* have the ending pattern of _____.
VCV	10. The C in the consonant-vowel patterns may signify a single consonant letter or a consonant digraph, but only one consonant phoneme. Since *ph* represents a single consonant phoneme, the nonsense word *sophe* has an ending pattern _____. (VCV, VCCV)
bāthé, blīthé, lāthé whīné, cūbé, phōné VCV	11. Mark each vowel in the following words with the proper diacritical mark: bathe blithe lathe whine cube phone All of the above have the consonant-vowel ending pattern _____.

When a one-syllable word has two vowels, one of which is the final *e,* the *e* is silent and the first vowel usually represents its long sound.	12. Write the generalization concerning vowel sounds illustrated by the words: *age, game, ice*
come, some *there*	13. It is well to remember that the generalization is very helpful but not infallible. Check the words in the following set which do not follow the generalization. (Is the final *e* silent? Does the first vowel "say its own name"?) come _____ place _____ these _____ some _____ there _____ late _____ clothe _____ fame _____
dance paste fence VCCV VCCV VCCV *waste pulse* VCCV VCCV	14. This generalization is of little value in helping to determine the vowel sound in words ending with the consonant-vowel pattern of VCCV, even when such words are of one syllable. Study the words below. Indicate the vowels which represent the long sound by using the macron. dance paste fence waste pulse _____ _____ _____ _____ _____ Write the ending pattern (begin with the vowel) under each of the words.

microscope
vaccinate
parade
bookcase
delete
 	
e
 	
e
 	
long
	15. Mark the last two vowels in each of the words at the right to show pronunciation. With these words in mind, our generalization might be extended to read:
	
	                        microscope
	                        vaccinate
	                        parade
	                        bookcase
	                        delete
	
	When a syllable has two vowels, one of which is a final _____,
	
	the _____ is silent and the first vowel usually represents its
	
	_____ sound.

v, I
 	
no   <u>*arrive*</u>
	16. All of the two- or more syllable words at the right have a final *e* which is silent.
	
	The consonant letter before the silent *e* in these words is either _____ or _____. Does the last syllable in each of these words follow the generalization we have been studying?
	
	_____
	
	Underline the words which do follow the generalization. Be sure you don't use an artificial pronunciation.
	
	                                 active
	                                   objective
	                                   motive
	                                   forgive
	                                   legislative
	                                   outlive
	                                   arrive
	                                   sterile
	                                   automobile

	17. When a syllable has two vowels, one of which is a final *e*, the *e* is silent and the first vowel usually represents the long (glided) sound.
	If we omit those words ending with *ve* and *le*, this generalization is of value in determining the vowel sounds in two- or more syllable words which have the ending pattern of VCe. The *ve* and *le* endings are too irregular to be depended upon.
	Which of the following endings is most apt to follow the generalization at the beginning of this frame?
ine	ale ive ave eve ine ole
long (or glided)	18. We have identified 5 of the vowel phonemes. These are the phonemes which represent the _____ sounds of the letters.
(All words below must have a silent, final *e*.)	We have also learned one generalization which gives a clue to that sound. Select one word for each of the five vowels to illustrate this generalization. Place a macron above the vowels selected.
stōle, remāke	shady one stole piece remake
extrēme, prīce,cūbe	extreme come price cube dance
consonant	19. We have noted that when we see the pattern of a single vowel followed by a single _____ and final *e*, the single vowel is likely to represent
long (glided)	its _____ sound.
so	20. Another situation in which we often find the vowel to be long is that of the "open syllable."
so lo *fe ver*	
ti ger	An open syllable is a syllable which ends with a vowel phoneme.
me *pa per*	Study the words at the right. Underline the open syllables, including open one-syllable words.
consonant	21. The first syllable of *sup pose* ends with a _____ phoneme.
	The second syllable of *sup pose* is not an open syllable because it does not
phoneme	end with a vowel _____. The last letter is a vowel, but it is (letter, phoneme)
silent	_____.

Right column word lists for frame 20:

so	*sup pose*
so lo	*fe ver*
pine	*ti ger*
me	*pa per*

yes $\bar{e}$ no r	22. Is the first syllable of *fe ver* an open syllable? _____ What key symbol represents the final phoneme of the first syllable? _____ Is the second syllable an open syllable? _____ What key symbol represents the final phoneme? _____
long	23. Study these words: <div style="text-align:center">hel <u>lo</u> <u>be</u> <u>me</u> ter <u>ti</u> ger</div>The underlined vowels represent their _____ sounds. <div style="text-align:center">(long, short)</div>

fā
       hē
       sī
       tō
open hū
glided (or long)
	24. Place a macron above the five vowels (*a, e, i, o, u*) which represent their glided sounds in the words at the right.
	
	We might generalize: A single vowel in an _____ syllable often represents its _____ sound.
	
	fa vor
	he
	si phon
	to tal
	hu man

sō̄ lō̄ rē make dī graph hā̄ lō̄ hel lō̄ do	25. Study the words at the right. Draw a line under the single vowels in the open syllables. Place a macron above those vowels you underlined which represent the long sound. Work carefully. You may find exceptions. *so lo* *re make* *di graph* *ha lo* *hel lo* *do*
e open	26. Although the *a* in *about* and the _____ in *debate* are single vowel letters in _____ syllables, they do not repre- <div style="text-align:center">(closed, open)</div>sent long sounds. We tend to shorten the vowel sounds in unaccented syllables. *a bout* *de bate*
long (glided)	27. The generalization has more application when we limit it to accented syllables: A single vowel in an open accented syllable usually represents its _____ sound. We will study this more fully later.

lō̄, lō̄	28. We should note, however, that sometimes single vowel letters in open <u>unaccented</u> syllables do represent the long sounds. *so'lo* *ha'lo* Two syllables from the words at the right which illustrate this are _____ from *solo* and _____ from *halo.* Mark the vowels in these unaccented syllables.
<u>pa</u> pa <u>to</u>	29. We should also note that not all vowels in open accented syllables represent long sounds. (Exceptions, exceptions!) Underline the syllables which are exceptions to the generalization: *no* *pa' pa* *to* *she* Single vowel letters in open accented syllables usually represent their long sounds.
a, e *i, o, u*	30. The previous frames contain examples of the five vowels, _____, _____, _____, _____, and _____, in which they represent their long sounds.
vowel	31. We have learned that the vowel *w* always appears with another _____ letter. Therefore, there would be no instances in which we could apply the <u>single-vowel open-syllable</u> generalization to the *w.*
bī *mī* *whī* *ī* *flī* *krī*	32. Let us examine the generalization with respect to the vowel *y.* Look at the words at the right. *by* _____ *my* _____ In each instance the *y* represents the phoneme we *why* _____ associate with the key symbol _____. Rewrite these *fly* _____ words. Use the key symbol we associate with each *cry* _____ vowel and consonant phoneme.
Some new dictionaries use the key symbol *ē* (long *e*). You may consider short *i* correct also.	33. Study the words at the right. Complete the generalization: *happy* *lucky* *baby* *windy* When *y* is the final letter of a two-syllable word, it represents the _____ sound of _____.
bī pas *sī pres* *dī namik*	34. *Y* is not always the final letter in a word. *by pass* _____ Study the words at the right. Rewrite them to *cy press* _____ show the pronunciation of the consonants and *dy namic* _____ of the vowels representing the long sounds.

cry *lucky*	35. If you agree that *y* represents the long sound of the *e* when it is the final and only vowel in the last syllable of a multisyllabic word, then the open-syllable generalization we have been studying applies to *a, e, i, o, u,* and *y*. The *y* would represent the sound of the long *i* in _____ and the <div align="center">*(cry, happy)*</div> long *e* in _____ . <div align="center">*(my, lucky)*</div>
A single vowel in an open, accented syllable often represents its long sound.	36. State the generalization which concerns a single vowel in an open syllable.

REVIEW 13

1. We have been studying five phonemes which represent the long sounds of the vowels: $\bar{a}$, _____, _____, _____, _____. We can show their pronunciation by placing a _____ (name of diacritical mark) over each of them.

2. *Y* can represent a long sound also, but it does not have a key symbol: it is a duplication of either the long _____ (as in *cry*) or the long _____ *(happy)*.

3. We have learned to recognize two patterns which may give clues as to the vowel sound in an unknown word. One is the vowel-consonant-silent _____ pattern (VCe). State the generalization:

4. The other is a single-vowel, open-syllable pattern: The single vowel in an _____ open syllable is often _____ .

5. Another way we can state the same generalization is: When the only vowel in a word or accented syllable comes at the _____ of the syllable, that vowel usually represents its _____ sound.

6. The long sounds of the vowels are easiest to recognize in known words because the name of the vowel is the same as the _____ it represents.

(See the Appendix for the answers to Review 13.)

Short Vowel Sounds

	ă (mad)　　ĕ (hen)　　ĭ (in)　　ŏ (hot)　　ŭ (sun)
	1. Thus far we have identified five of the vowel sounds. We call them "long" or glided sounds.
	We distinguish them (as in the dictionary) from other sounds by placing
macrons	_____ over them.
	2. The breve (˘) is a diacritical mark used to indicate a specific pronunciation of each of a second group of vowels. Its linguistic relationship to "short" can be noted in such words as "abbreviate" and "brevity." It is the custom, in phonics, to call the vowel sound whose key symbol contains a breve a "short" vowel sound.
short	The vowels in the words at the top of this section represent the _____
	(long, short)
breve	sounds. Each key symbol consists of a vowel marked with a _____.
	3. Because, in actuality, these sounds are not held for a shorter period of time than certain other vowel phonemes, some prefer to call them unglided phonemes.
short	If you write "unglided" and this text gives the answer as "_____" (or vice versa), you may count your answer correct.
ĭ, ŏ, ŭ	4. The key symbols which identify the vowels when they represent their short sounds are: ă, ĕ, _____, _____, _____. Reading would be easier if five additional characters representing these _____ were added to our
phonemes	alphabet.　　(letters, phonemes)
m, a	5. Pronounce the word mad. Listen for three phonemes, the consonant phoneme represented by _____, the vowel phoneme represented by _____, and the
consonant, d	_____ phoneme represented by _____. Pronounce the vowel
apple	sound alone. The same sound is heard in _____.
	(apple, far)
măd	6. Pronounce the vowel phoneme in mad. Rewrite mad using key symbols: _____. Pronounce the following words. Circle those whose vowel phoneme is the same as that in mad.
ran, grab, tack	ran　all　car　above　grab　tack　paw

3 hĕn	7. There are _____ phonemes in *hen*. Listen for the vowel phoneme as you say *hen* aloud. Rewrite *hen* using key symbols to indicate its pronunciation. _____
mĕt, kĕg, wĕtter	8. Mark with a breve each of the vowels in the words below which represents the same vowel phoneme heard in *hen*. *feed met rib keg wetter reward* If you find this difficult, pronounce the vowel phoneme heard in *hen*, then pronounce each word, substituting that sound for each vowel phoneme.
3 rĕd	9. Read this sentence aloud: *I read a book yesterday.* How many phonemes do you hear when you say *read* in the sentence above? _____ Rewrite *read*, using a key symbol to indicate each phoneme. _____ You have written in code. Anyone who knows the code can pronounce *read* correctly without a sentence to clarify it.
pĭn, pīné, rĭft, sĭtē or sĭtĭ	10. Pronounce *in*. Now say the vowel phoneme. Rewrite the following words using key symbols to code <u>each</u> phoneme: *pin* _____ *pine* _____ *rift* _____ *city* _____

3
 	
odd
	11. Pronounce *hot*. It contains _____ phonemes. The vowel pho-
	                                    (How many?)
	neme sounds the same as that in _____.
	                                    (boy, odd)

lĭp, tŏp, pŏp, găp, grăph, pŏd key symbols	12. Indicate the pronunciation of each short (unglided) vowel sound by using the correct diacritical mark in these words: *lip top note pop gap graph pod probe* The vowel letters with the marks you placed above them are the _____ _____ for the phonemes they represent.
sŭn jŭmp, ŭs, rŭnt, cŭp	13. Pronounce *sun*. Rewrite it using key symbols. _____ Pro-nounce the vowel sound alone. Place the correct diacritical marks above all the vowels in the following words which represent the same sound as the vowel phoneme in *sun*. *jump cube use us runt cup house*

short *fĕnce* *pŭg*	14. Pronounce the vowel phoneme represented by the vowel in each of the words in the first column at the right. Each vowel represents its _____ phoneme. Now pronounce the vowel phoneme in each of the words in the second column. Place a breve above each vowel in the second column which represents its unglided sound. Check carefully. <table><tr><td>1</td><td>2</td></tr><tr><td>*an*</td><td>*car*</td></tr><tr><td>*fed*</td><td>*fence*</td></tr><tr><td>*pin*</td><td>*pine*</td></tr><tr><td>*hot*</td><td>*cow*</td></tr><tr><td>*cup*</td><td>*pug*</td></tr></table>
rĕdē or *rĕdĭ* *sĕd* *sĕnts* *ĕnd*	15. Pronounce the words at the right. Listen carefully for the vowel phonemes. Rewrite each word, using the key symbols which indicate the sounds we associate with the vowel and consonant phonemes. *ready* _____ *said* _____ *cents* _____ *end* _____
open phoneme	16. We call a syllable which ends with a vowel phoneme an _____ syllable. We call a syllable which ends with a consonant _____ a closed syllable.
closed	17. Look at the words below. Are these one-syllable words closed or open? _____ an fed pin hot cup
vowel, consonant	18. The most common vowel-consonant pattern is that of CVC in which the V represents its short sound. There are many one-syllable words and many accented syllables in multisyllable words which follow this pattern. These words and syllables are made of an initial consonant, a middle _____, and a final _____.
rang, this, rab bit, big	19. The C in the pattern may represent a digraph or a blend. Circle the syllables (or one-syllable words) which have the CVC pattern. rang this rab bit be side a gain big
closed closed	20. Syllables with the CVC pattern are _____ syllables; those (closed, open) with the VC pattern (like *an*) are _____ syllables.

short (unglided) c	21. VC, in which the vowel represents the _____ sound as in *an*, is also a common pattern. It functions the same as the CV_____ pattern.
short (unglided) breve	22. The CVC and the VC patterns give clues to the pronunciation of unknown words. In both cases we would expect the vowel to represent the _____ sound. To indicate the pronunciation of the vowel, we place a _____ above it.
sĕt, lŏt yes (Blends and digraphs are considered as C's.)	23. Do the vowels in all CVC patterns represent the short sound? Study the following words and syllables. *far ther long set lot her* Do all of them have the CVC pattern? _____ Mark the vowels which represent the short sounds with breves. Work carefully.
yes *Dăn kĕpt hĭs pŏp gŭn.*	24. The key words given at the beginning of this section will help us remember the phoneme for each vowel. A sentence which contains each of the "short" vowel phonemes may be easier to remember. Would the sentence below furnish a key word for each of the short vowel phonemes? _____ (Check each word with the set at the beginning of this section.) Mark the vowels with breves. *Dan kept his pop gun.*
4 *Năn's pĕt ĭs nŏt fŭn.* *Săm's nĕt ĭs nŏt cŭt.* *Săd Tĕd ĭn hŏt hŭt.* *All mĕn ĭn hŏt bŭs.*	25. Look at the groups of words below. Mark the vowels which represent the short sound. No. _____ is not a good key phrase. (1) *Nan's pet is not fun.* (2) *Sam's net is not cut.* (3) *Sad Ted in hot hut.* (4) *All men in hot bus.*
short *don't, bird*	26. One vowel in a closed syllable (or in a one-syllable word) usually represents its _____ sound. With your key sentence in mind, check the vowel phonemes in the following words. Which words do not have the short vowel phoneme? *clap don't skin sick trust fed bend bird*

yes *but ton* *pen cil* yes	27. Study these words carefully. Is each syllable a closed syllable? *but ton* _____ Write the closed syllables here: *pen cil* Is there a single vowel in each syllable? _____
unaccented	28. We might expect that we can properly indicate the pronuncia- *but' ton* tion of each of the vowels with a breve. If you pronounce the *pen' cil* words too carefully—that is, artificially—you might indicate their pronunciation that way. Say a sentence aloud containing the word *button,* then one with *pencil.* You will notice that the vowel in the _____ syllable represents more of (accented, unaccented) an *"uh"* sound and not the phonemes you hear in the words *hot* and *in.*
closed short	29. The generalization for the short vowel phoneme is most useful when it is stated: A single vowel in an accented _____ syllable usually represents the _____ sound of the vowel.

vowel
 	
short
 	
i
	30. We have noted the sounds represented by *a, e, i, o, u.* How *myth*
	about the *y*? *sys tem*
	                                             rhythm
	Study the words at the right. Each contains a _____ *y*
	                             (consonant, vowel)
	within the syllable. The *y* represents the _____ sound
	                             (long, short)
	of the letter _____.

fĭt
      rŏt
      păn
      pĕg
(If you have an error,
check the sound care-
fully again.)
	31. Let us review the short sounds of the vowels. Check the *hate* *put*
	words at the right against the key words you have learned. *want* *fit*
	Place a breve above each of the vowels which represents the *pan* *rot*
	short sound of that vowel. *peg* *cute*

short	32. We can expect that single vowels in closed accented syllables will usually represent _____ sounds. Remember that all one-syllable words are considered accented syllables.

yes no long, silent	33. Are the vowels in the words at the right single vowels in closed syllables? _____ Do they follow the CVC generalization? _____ An exception to the generalization is found in words in which the *i* is followed by *gh*. The *i* represents the _____ sound and the *gh* is _____ in such words. *sight* *might* *right* *fight*
yes long	34. Do the words at the right illustrate another exception? _____ We find that when *i* or *o* is followed by *ld*, the vowel usually represents the _____ sound. *child* *wild* *old* *cold*
long short	35. Study the "final *e*" words at the right. You will recall that, when there is a single consonant letter between the vowel and final *e*, the vowel generally represents the _____ sound. Now note that in words ending with *nce* or *dge* the first vowel phoneme is _____ . *fence* *budge* *sludge* *dance*

short   *pīne*   *cūte*
        rāte   *strīpe*
        kīte   *pāle*
        hāte   *āte*
 	
long
	36. All the vowels at the right represent the _____ sounds. Check each one to make sure.
	
	Now attach a silent *e* at the end of each word to see what happens. To show the new pronunciation, mark the first vowel in each of the new words you've made with the appropriate diacritical mark.
	
	The vowels now represent their _____ sounds. *pin* *cut*
	rat *strip*
	kit *pal*
	hat *at*

e pronunciation (or sound)	37. We can see that the silent _____ at the end of a word has a purpose. It changes the meaning of the word as well as the _____ of the word. *cut* *cute* *strip* *stripe*
     bend *pin*	38. Now take time to study your own dictionary. Look up *bend.* Does the breve appear above the *e* in the pronunciation guide? Since the unglided vowel sound is so common, many dictionaries indicate the pronunciation of all short sounds with the letter alone (no diacritical mark). How would the pronunciation of *bend* be shown in these dictionaries? _____ Of *pin?* _____

$\bar{a}\ \bar{e}\ \bar{\imath}\ \bar{o}\ \bar{u}$	39. Pronounce the five "long vowel phonemes." Write the key symbols we use to represent them: ＿＿＿ ＿＿＿ ＿＿＿ ＿＿＿ ＿＿＿.
$\breve{a}\ \breve{e}\ \breve{\imath}\ \breve{o}\ \breve{u}$	40. Write the key symbols we are using in this text to represent the "short vowel phonemes." ＿＿＿ ＿＿＿ ＿＿＿ ＿＿＿ ＿＿＿ Pronounce the "short vowel phonemes." Can you say them as rapidly as the long vowel phonemes? Practice them. Since they are so common, you should be very familiar with them.

REVIEW 14

1. Can you state the major generalizations concerning long and short vowel sounds?

   a. Write the generalization which applies to the words at the right.

   net
   on

   b. State the generalization that applies to the vowel sounds in the words at the right.

   pine
   home

   c. Write the generalization which applies to the underlined syllables at the right.

   go
   relay

2. We are studying the vowel phonemes which are represented by a single letter. We have learned to associate 10 of the 19 vowel phonemes with their key pronunciation symbols. Mark the vowels to indicate their pronunciation:

   bite   bit   can   cane   pet   Pete   us   fuse   pock   poke

3. Pronounce the words at the right.

   a. Place a C behind each word which ends with a consonant phoneme.

   b. Place a V behind each word which ends with a vowel phoneme.

   c. Indicate the pronunciation of the final phoneme by writing the key symbol. If it consists of a blend, use only the symbol which represents the final phoneme in the blend.

   d. Underline the words in which the final syllable is an open syllable.

   dine   table
   tack   hello
   ledge   he
   antique   tight
   watch   enough

70   **Vowels**

4. We expect the single letter *g* to represent its hard sound, except when it is followed by _____, _____, or _____.

(See Appendix for the answers to Review 14.)

The Schwa

<table>
<tr><td></td><td colspan="2">ə (comma, label, pupil, button, circus)</td></tr>
<tr>
<td>a, e, i, o, u</td>
<td>1. Say the words at the right aloud. Listen to the phoneme represented by the underlined letter. When you say the words slowly and distinctly (and artificially), they may sound quite different from one another. But when these words are used in ordinary speech, the underlined part represents a very soft "uh."

The letters which represent the uh sound in the words at the right are _____, _____, _____, _____, _____.</td>
<td>comma
label
pupil
button
circus</td>
</tr>
<tr>
<td>ə</td>
<td colspan="2">2. It is becoming more and more common for dictionaries to indicate that "soft" vowel sound found in unaccented syllables with a schwa (ə).

The pronunciation is shown by the sign _____ (an inverted e).</td>
</tr>
<tr>
<td>blend</td>
<td colspan="2">3. And how is the word schwa pronounced? The sch grapheme in schwa represents the phoneme we associate with the key symbol sh.

The sh and the consonant w form a _____. The a represents an ah
(digraph, blend)
sound.</td>
</tr>
<tr>
<td>commə
labəl
pupəl
buttən
circəs</td>
<td>4. Rewrite these words to show the pronunciation of the vowel in the unaccented syllable.

Without the schwa, each of these vowels would need a separate diacritical mark.</td>
<td>com′ ma _____
la′ bel _____
pu′ pil _____
but′ ton _____
cir′ cus _____</td>
</tr>
<tr>
<td>schwa

bā′kən</td>
<td colspan="2">5. The vowel phoneme in many unaccented syllables is shown by the _____.

Study the word below. Rewrite it, indicating the sound of each letter.

 ba′ con _____ </td>
</tr>
</table>

ĕləfənt *līən* *ănəməl* *hĭpəpŏtəməs* Check all: *a, e, i, o, u*	6. Say the words at the right in a natural manner. Rewrite them, using key symbols to indicate each of the phonemes. Check the vowels which can represent the schwa phoneme: *a* ____ *e* ____ *i* ____ *o* ____ *u* ____ elephant _____ lion _____ animal _____ hippopotamus _____
unaccented	7. The use of the *schwa* for each vowel which represents the short *"uh"* sound, along with the frequent use of the short *i* (*ĭ*), has simplified pronunciation keys greatly. Almost all vowels in _____ syllables represent one of these two (accented, unaccented) short, soft sounds.
second	8. Let us examine the word *deteriorate*. One dictionary indicates the pronunciation as *dē̇ tēr i ȯ rāt;* another as *dĭ tĭr ĭ ə rāt*. The _____ (first, second) is following the trend of making greater use of the *ĭ* and the *ə* to indicate these two soft phonemes regardless of the original spelling.
reasonable, honor	9. These words are written to show their pronunciation. What are the words? *rē'zən ə bəl* _____ *ŏn'ər* _____

pĕn'səl, mī'nəs
 	
sō'fə, mī'krəskōp
	10. Rewrite the words below to show pronunciation. Omit the silent letters.
	
	    pen'cil _____ *mi'nus* _____
	
	    so'fa _____ *mi'croscope* _____

er *bĭgər*	11. Although the word part *er* has only a touch of a vowel sound, the schwa is used with the *r* to indicate the pronunciation of the word part _____. Thus the key symbols of *bigger* are _____ (Check your dictionary to see how it treats this word part.)

plī' ərz, plĕzh' ər
 	
kwĭv' ər, drān' ĭj
 	
kō' kō, zī' lə fōn'
	12. Are you ready to code some more difficult words? Rewrite the following to show pronunciation:
	
	    pli' ers _____ *pleas' ure* _____
	
	    quiv' er _____ *drain' age* _____
	
	    co' coa _____ *xy' lo phone'* _____

sĭm'fə nē (or nĭ) *ĭ mŭl'shən, dĭf'ə kŭlt* *ăn tēk'* (You may have some variations; all dictionaries do not agree.)	13. Now let's try some difficult words. Rewrite these words to show pronunciation. They should be written as they might appear in parenthesis following the boldface entry word in the dictionary. To avoid artificial pronunciation, check each one by saying it in a sentence. *sym'pho ny* _____ *e mul'sion* _____ *dif'fi cult* _____ *an tique'* _____
short *i*	14. The first vowel in *emulsion* represents the _____ _____ phoneme. This use represents the trend toward simplification. Some dictionaries use the modified macron ($\perp$) to indicate the pronunciation of the first vowel. It is not *ē*. Try it in a sentence to check this. Now try it using *ĭ* as a guide in pronouncing the first syllable.
i mul'shən (or i mul'shun)	15. It is necessary to note that various dictionaries indicate pronunciation in different ways. We must study the pronunciation key of the particular dictionary we use. For example, many dictionaries indicate the pronunciation of all short sounds with the letter and no diacritical mark. The pronunciation of *emulsion* is written _____.

REVIEW 15

1. The key symbol which is used to represent many of the vowel phonemes in unaccented syllables is called a _____. It resembles an inverted _____.

2. It is very useful because _____.

3. *ər* is used to indicate the pronunciation of a word part in _____.
                                                                      (river, erase)

4. These words are written to show their pronunciation. How are they correctly spelled?

    rē gəl   hănd mād   sĕl ə brāt   kăr əl   ĕs tə māt   sə spĕn shən

    (See Appendix for the answers to Review 15.)

Other Single Vowels

	â (dare) û (hurt) ä (arm) ô (tall)
5 schwa phoneme	1. Thus far we have identified eleven vowel phonemes using only _____ vowel (How many?) letters and a _____. We can readily tell which _____ is represented when diacritical (letter, phoneme) marks are used, as in a dictionary, glossary, or other pronunciation guide.
unglided (short)	2. But we have also examined patterns common to the English language so that we can make a reasonable guess as to the sound of certain vowels. For example, we expect the vowel in the pattern CVC to represent its _____ sound.
fad	3. If that vowel in the CVC pattern were *a*, we would expect that *a* to represent the same sound as the vowel phoneme heard in _____. (said, car, ball, fad, date, caw)
glided, silent	4. We expect the first vowel in the ending pattern VCe to represent its _____ sound and the final *e* to be _____.
sew	5. If the first vowel in the VCe ending pattern is an *o*, we expect it to represent the same vowel phoneme as that heard in _____. (done, gone, boy, sew)
schwa *sofa*	6. A vowel in an unaccented syllable could reasonably be expected to represent the sound we associate with an unglided *i* or with the _____. The *ə* would identify the vowel phoneme in the last syllable of _____. (sofa, remit, require, insect)
graphemes	7. There are still other vowel phonemes. Some are influenced by the consonant following the vowel. We will identify these vowel phonemes and suggest a key word by which each can be remembered. Each may be represented by a variety of spellings, in other words, by a variety of _____. (sounds, graphemes)

r	8. Let's examine the vowel phoneme in the key word *dare*. The key symbol we will use to represent this phoneme is â. We can hardly separate it from the following consonant phoneme, so we call it _____ -controlled. 　*(r, l, w)*
yes 6	9. Study the words at the right. Pronounce each word aloud. Is the vowel phoneme the same in each word? _____ . In these examples, one vowel phoneme is represented by _____ graphemes. （How many?)　*chair* *bare* *their* *there* *wear* *prayer*
ai, a, ei, e, ea, ay	10. Underline the graphemes which represent the same vowel phoneme as that heard in *dare*. They represent vowel phonemes, so do not underline the controlling consonant. 　　*chair　bare　their　there　wear　prayer*
kâr, whâr, fârē *shâr, flâr, băt* *bat*	11. Rewrite the words below, using the key symbols to indicate the pronunciation of consonants and vowels. Omit silent letters. *care* _____　　*where* _____　　*fairy* _____ *share* _____　　*flair* _____　　*bat* _____ The word out of place in this list is _____ .
air, anchor, lair *pile, Gary, rarity* *race, civic, their* 　　　or *there*	12. These words are written to show pronunciation. Spell them correctly: âr _____　　ăng′ kər _____　　lâr _____ pīl _____　　Gâr′ ĭ _____　　râr′ ə tĭ _____ rās _____　　sĭv′ ĭk _____　　t͟hâr _____
r　　*i* 　　*e* 　　*ea* 　　*o* 　　*u* 　　*y*	13. Another vowel phoneme which is *r*-controlled is the one heard in *hurt*. In fact, it is impossible to separate it from the _____ . Say the words at the right. What graphemes represent the vowel phoneme heard in *hurt* as shown by the words at the right?　*thirst* *term* *learn* *worm* *purr* *myrtle*

Vowels　75

thûrst, tûrm, lûrn *wûrm, pûrr, mûrtle*	14. Rewrite the words above using the *û* to show the pronunciation of that part of the word. _____ _____ _____ _____ _____ _____
wûrkər, wûrkt, snâr	15. Note that this phoneme is not the same as that heard as a separate syllable, generally a suffix, as in *farmer, lower,* etc. We will identify this separate syllable by *ər.* Rewrite the following words to show pronunciation: *worker* _____ *worked* _____ *snare* _____
băngkər *sōljər* *dûrt* *prâr*	16. Rewrite the words at the right to show their pronunciation. *banker* _____ *soldier* _____ *dirt* _____ *prayer* _____
several different *hurt*	17. The phoneme which we associate with the key symbol *û* may be represented by _____ graphemes. The key word chosen to help us (only one, several different) remember this phoneme is _____.
several different, *dare*	18. The phoneme which we associate with the key symbol *â* may be represented by _____ graphemes. Its key word is _____. (only one, several different)
graphemes (or spellings)	19. The phoneme which we will identify with the key symbol *ä* and the key word *arm* may be confusing because of regional differences in pronunciation. It is represented by many different letters and combinations of letters. Dictionaries reveal anywhere from 3 to 11 different _____ which represent this phoneme.
ä	20. Pronounce the words at the right. If you do not hear the vowel phoneme you hear in *arm,* your pronunciation is simply reflecting a regional difference. You are not wrong. Now pronounce them so that you can hear the phoneme we represent by the key symbol _____ in each one.

father
calm
hearth
sergeant
bazaar

a, al, ea, e, aa	21. In the words below underline the graphemes which represent the phoneme we identify by ä. Include the silent letters which could be considered a part of the grapheme. father calm hearth sergeant bazaar
fär, shwä, pläzə bäm, gärd, dâr	22. If you cannot agree with the pronunciation, use your dictionary. It may reflect the pronunciation of your region. Use the key symbols to show the pronunciation of these words: far _____ schwa _____ plaza _____ balm _____ guard _____ dare _____
kärnāshən, kärbən, bâr kârət, kāk, hûrt	23. Rewrite these words to show pronunciation: carnation _____ carbon _____ bear _____ carrot _____ cake _____ hurt _____
raw, caught, walk, broad fought, tall, order	24. Pronounce tall. Listen to the vowel phoneme. We will represent this phoneme with the key symbol ô. Say the words below. Check those in which you hear the phoneme heard in tall. raw _____ caught _____ walk _____ broad _____ bead _____ fought _____ tall _____ order _____ Some of the answers here may also be affected by regional variations in pronunciation. Check your dictionary.
aw, au, al, oa, ou, a, o	25. What graphemes above represent the vowel phoneme heard in tall? _____
rô, kôt, wôk, brôd, bēd, fôt, tôl, ôrder	26. Rewrite the above words using key symbols to indicate pronunciation. _____ _____ _____ _____ _____ _____ _____ _____
3, 1, 3, 2, 4 1, 3, 4, 4	27. Let us review: Four single-vowel phonemes are represented by the underlined letters at the right. 1. â dare 2. ä arm 3. ô tall 4. û hurt Indicate the pronunciation of the underlined vowels in the words below by using the number of the word in which the vowel has the same pronunciation. fault ____ despair ____ Utah ____ sergeant ____ term ____ there ____ broad ____ courage ____ worm ____

	28. There are a few broad generalizations which may be of some help in determining the pronunciation of these vowels in unknown words. *car* *farmer* *furl* *fir* *orb*
r	If the only vowel letter in a word or syllable is followed by *r*, the vowel will be affected by that _____. Say the words at the right.
short	The vowel sounds are neither long nor _____. They are
r	almost lost in the consonant letter _____.

	29. If the only vowel in a word or syllable is an *a* followed by *l* or *w*, *lawn* *saw* *late* *fall* *install*
l, w	the *a* is affected by that _____ or _____. Study the words at the
late	right. Which word does not belong in the list? _____ Do
no	any of the others represent the long or short sound of *a*?_____ Does the *a* followed by *l* represent the same sound as the *a* followed
yes	by *w?* _____
	Again, regional variations in the pronunciation of these words may cause you some difficulty.

REVIEW 16

1. We have been studying the vowel phonemes which can be represented by single-vowel key symbols. The first group of five (example, *make*) we labeled the _____ vowel phonemes. Write their key symbols: _____.

2. The second group of five (example, *wet*) we labeled _____ vowel phonemes. Write their key symbols: _____.

3. The third (example, *comma*) was given a key symbol not in the alphabet, called the _____.
   This key symbol, _____, represents each of the vowels when they have the sound heard in _____.
   (happy, anew)

4. That left us with four additional single-vowel phonemes which cannot be grouped except for the influence on them of the phoneme _____ the vowel. We found that they were affected by
   (following, preceding)
   phonemes represented by the _____, _____, and _____.

5. The key words for these vowel phonemes can be placed in the following sentence. Fill in the blanks and mark the vowels.

   The _____ player does not _____ to _____ his _____.

   (See Appendix for the answers to Review 16.)

Diphthongs

oi (oil)   *ou (house)*

consonant	1. We have been studying the vowel phonemes which are represented by single vowel letters. We will now turn our attention to those which are represented by combinations of letters. Say *oil*. The word *oil* is composed of two phonemes: one vowel and one _____ .
l	They are represented by the graphemes *oi* and _____ .

boil *house* *cow* *boy* *coin* *employ* *mouse*	2. The *oi* functions as one phoneme called a diphthong. Although the diphthong is to be considered a single-vowel phoneme, it resembles a "glide" from one sound to another. Examine the words at the right. Underline the grapheme in each word which represents the diphthong. Say each word out loud. Listen for the "glide."	*boil* *house* *cow* *boy* *coin* *employ* *mouse*

diphthongs (Check the spelling.)	3. A study of phonetics (the science of speech sounds) would show that many single-letter vowels are actually diphthongs. They represent more than a single sound. Note the gliding sound of the *u* in *use*. You may be using "glided" rather than "long" for this vowel phoneme. We will call only the two-letter gliding combinations _____ .

diphthong	4. In this study we have made the arbitrary statement that there are 44 phonemes. It really is not that simple! Say *few*. Is the vowel phoneme equivalent to the phoneme heard at the beginning of *use*, or should we consider *ew* a separate diphthong, not a duplication of any single-vowel phoneme? Our decision is to consider that *few* = $f\bar{u}$. So we will <u>not</u> call *ew* a _____ .

oi, ou	5. It seems most helpful to classify only two of the vowel phonemes as diphthongs. These are the vowel sounds heard in *oil* and *house*. The _____ and the _____ then represent two of the 44 speech sounds in our language.

yes *oi, oy*	6. Say the words at the right. Does each word contain a diphthong? _____ We note that each diphthong is represented by two graphemes. What graphemes represent the vowel phoneme heard in *oil*? _____ and _____	*oil* *boy* *house* *cow*

ou *ow*	7. What graphemes represent the vowel phoneme heard in *house?* _____ and _____
diphthongs	8. We will use *oi* and *ou* as key symbols to represent the two phonemes we call _____.
oi *joi*	9. The key symbol for the vowel phoneme heard in *joy* is _____. Rewrite *joy* showing its pronunciation. _____
ou *kloun*	10. The key symbol for the vowel phoneme heard in *clown* is _____. Rewrite *clown* to show its pronunciation. _____

two, two
 	
 two, no
 	
 ou, oi
	11. We are recognizing _____ diphthongs. Each has _____ spellings. The key
	         (How many?) (How many?)
	 symbol for each diphthong is composed of _____ letters with _____ dia-
	                         (How many?) (one, two, no)
	 critical marks. These letters will be either _____ or _____ because they are
	                               (ou, ow) (oi, oy)
	 the key symbols. We find them used in most dictionaries for pronunciation purposes.

koi
       ĕmploi
       broil
 snow   *snō*
       kou
	12. Study the words at the right. Rewrite them, *coy* _____
	 using key symbols to indicate the pronunciation *employ* _____
	 of all the phonemes. Underline the diphthongs. *broil* _____
	 There is no diphthong in _____. *snow* _____
	  cow _____

p<u>ow</u>der, pr<u>ou</u>d, h<u>ow</u>, s<u>oi</u>l	13. Underline the diphthongs in the following words. Work with care. The *ou* and *ow* often represent other phonemes. Be sure you underline only those which have the vowel phonemes found in *oil* and *house.* *powder* *proud* *course* *how* *soil* *courage* *gracious*
short	14. The *ous* ending, as in *gracious,* is more likely to represent the phonemes we associate with the key symbols _____ *u* and *s* (or the schwa (long, short) and *s*) than with the diphthong *ou* and the *s.* If we do not have the word in our speaking vocabulary, however, it is very difficult to determine whether the *ou (ow)* is a diphthong or not.

REVIEW 17

1. Two of the 44 phonemes are classified as diphthongs. What are the key symbols of these two diphthongs?

   _____, _____

2. The diphthongs are _____ phonemes.
   (vowel, consonant)

3. Which of these words contain diphthongs?

   grow   plow   through

4. Use key symbols to show the pronunciation of the following words (omit silent letters):

   blow _____   pounce _____

   (See the Appendix for the answers to Review 17.)

Vowel Digraphs

rāi̸n	1. The second category of phonemes represented by two-letter vowels is that of the vowel <u>digraph</u>. Study the word *rain*.
	Underline the pair of vowels. Indicate the silent vowel by drawing a slash through it. Mark the long vowel.
3, r, a, n	*Rain* has _____ phonemes represented by _____, long _____, and _____. (How many?)
rāi̸l sāy̸ macron pēa̸ch fēe̸d silent cōa̸t	2. Study the words at the right. Underline the pair of vowels in each word. As you say each word, place a _____ over the first (macron, breve) vowel. Indicate that the second vowel is _____ by drawing a slash through it. *rail* *say* *peach* *feed* *coat*
long, silent	3. A syllable must have one and only one vowel phoneme. Many syllables (and one-syllable words) have two vowel letters. Note the words at the right. In these cases, the first vowel represents its _____ sound and the second vowel is _____. *rain* *feed* *hue* *foe*
rain, feed, may, foe	4. A syllable may contain 2 vowels, but unless they are next to each other, they are not digraphs. Which of these words contain digraphs? rain feed pine may foe rose delete

2 long silent	5. We can make a generalization about digraphs in the words you have studied. When _____ vowels appear together in a syllable (or one-syllable word), the first usually represents its _____ sound and the second is _____.
cēasé, plāý, plāín, ēách	6. Mark each vowel in these words to show the pronunciation. <p align="center">cease play plain each</p>
diphthong	7. The generalization does not apply to *boil* because *oi* is a _____: it has a distinctive sound of its own.

<u>bail</u>
no   <u>toe</u>
 	
long
silent
	8. Study the words at the right. *bail*
	    said
	Is the generalization concerning vowel digraphs always true? _____ *toe*
	Underline the words which follow the generalization: *foot*
	    food
	When two vowels appear together in a word or syllable, the first *piece*
	usually represents the _____ sound, and the second is _____.

ai, oa, ee, ea, ay	9. There are many exceptions to this generalization. It can only be used as a clue to the possible pronunciation of a word. However, there are some digraphs which follow the generalization more consistently than others. The digraphs which are most consistent appear in these words: *maintain, boat, keep, each, dismay.* The digraphs which follow the generalization a greater percentage of the time are _____, _____, _____, _____, _____.
sĕd	10. However, even these are not without exception. The digraph listed first *(ai)* appears in *said.* Rewrite *said* using needed diacritical marks to show its pronunciation. <p align="center">*said* _____</p>
digraphs sounded	11. We have classified the vowel combinations in the words at the *jail* right as _____. We might have considered them phonemes *coat* represented by single letters because in each case only one of the *need* *leaf* letters is _____. *gray* <p align="center">(sounded, silent)</p>

long	**12.** We choose not to consider these under the classification of vowels which represent their _____ sounds because they are not nearly as (long, short) regular as those represented by the VCe pattern.

	i *e*	**13.** If they were as regular, we could form a gener- *pine* _____ _____
	o *e*	alization to include both types: *rose* _____ _____
	o *a*	When there are two vowel letters in a word or *boat* _____ _____
long	*e* *e*	syllable, the first usually represents its _____ *jeep* _____ _____
silent		sound and the second is _____.

For the words at the right, place the vowel which represents the long sound in the first column following the word and the silent letter in the second.

---

o͞o (food)   o͝o (hook)

14. There are two digraphs which do represent phonemes not already represented by a single-letter grapheme. Pronounce the vowel phoneme heard in *food,* then the vowel phoneme in *hook.* The macron must be lengthened to cover both *o*'s in *food* to show the pronunciation.

hook   The breve is lengthened to cover the two *o*'s of _____. These marks are different from those which show the long or short sounds of single vowels.

---

fo͝ot, mo͞ose̸, to͝ok, lo͝ok, so͞on, po͞ol, wo͝od, to͞oth, lo͞ose̸	**15.** Using *food* and *hook* as key words to aid you, mark the words below to show the pronunciation: *foot* *moose* *took* *look* *soon* *pool* *wood* *tooth* *loose*

---

goose	**16.** When you see a double-*o* in an unknown word, the only clue to pronunciation is that it most often represents the o͞o as in _____. (goose, book) You may wish to choose other key words to help you remember the phonemes. *Hook* serves as a good key word for the phoneme we represent by o͝o if we see a resemblance between an elongated breve and a hook! (a pla̅te of fo͞od?)

---

blŭd
sto͝od
zo͞o
flŭd
dro͞op
	17. But not all *oo*'s represent the sounds heard in *food* and *hook.* Rewrite the words at the right to show the correct pronunciation of each. *blood* _____
	
	                                                 stood _____
	
	                                                 zoo _____
	
	                                                 flood _____
	
	                                                 droop _____

REVIEW 18

1. We have been studying the phonemes represented by vowel letters. First, we studied phonemes represented by single vowel letters, putting the greatest emphasis on the _____ (hope) and _____ (hop) sounds.

2. We have noted that there are exceptions to any _____ we make concerning these sounds.

3. We have also noted that the single vowel letters represent other sounds. We have recognized the trend to use the _____ to designate the soft sound of the vowel in unaccented _____.

4. We have also studied vowel phonemes represented by two vowel letters. We identified two _____ phonemes, *oi* and _____.

5. We noted that most of the two-letter combinations called _____ (as in *rain*) represent phonemes already identified in the single-letter category.

6. However, we discovered two phonemes represented by one vowel digraph, the _____ digraph (as *food, hook*). Mark these words to show pronunciation:

    ooze   moon   rook   gloom   brook   hood

7. The generalizations we have studied in connection with these vowel phonemes should aid in the pronunciation of words we do not recognize. The words below are nonsense words. Take a chance that the vowel phonemes follow the rules even in unaccented syllables or have their most common sound. Mark every vowel in these "words" to show pronunciation:

    me   lepe   pha   tog   rel   no   pho   ot   dlaif   rhoos

8. We have learned that, for practical purposes in the teaching of reading, there are _____ consonant and vowel phonemes in the American-English language. We have now identified all of them!

(See the Appendix for the answers to Review 18)

IV. A Review Of The Phonemes

phonemes (or sounds)	1. Our written language is not based on pictorial representations of objects or ideas. It is phonetic language in that there is a relationship between the letters of the alphabet and the _____ of the spoken language.
consonants	2. In fact, many of the _____ are fairly reliable as to sound. (consonants, vowels)
phonemes letters	3. However, there are so many inconsistencies in the sound-letter relationship that the English language is not an easy one to learn to read. If it were a consistent, strictly phonetic language, then (1) there would be one and only one letter to represent each of the _____ of the spoken language; (2) there would be one and only one phoneme represented by each of the _____ of the alphabet.
26 phonemes phonemes sh silent	4. The truth of the matter is: (1) A letter may represent more than one sound. For example, each vowel represents several sounds. Our alphabet has _____ letters (and some of them are useless) to represent the 44 _____. (2) The same sound may be represented by more than one letter. The 44 _____ are represented by 251 different graphemes. For example, we spell the first consonant phoneme we hear in *chute* (key symbol: _____) in 14 different ways! (3) A letter may represent no sound. Almost any letter may, at some time or another, be _____.

spoken	5. We have identified the 44 phonemes which, for all practical purposes in the teaching of reading, make up the sounds of our _____ language. <div align="center">(spoken, written)</div>
symbol *j*	6. We have designated a key symbol for each of these phonemes to serve as our pronunciation guide. These key pronunciation symbols, then, provide us with a one-to-one correspondence between sound and _____. For example, we use the _____ to symbolize the sound heard in *jam,* even though it may be represented by *g* as in *gentle, d* as in *graduate,* or *dg* as in *judgment.*
key symbols	7. Let's review, through the following outline, the 44 phonemes we have identified and the _____ _____ we have designated for each. Study and make responses as indicated. When choices appear in parentheses, underline the correct answer. For example, there are 44 (phonemes, graphemes).

REVIEW OUTLINE

I. CONSONANT PHONEMES

		Key Symbol
	A. Represented by a single consonant letter	
bat	*b* as in (*bat, numb*). (Select the word in which *b* represents the sound we associate with its key symbol.)	1. *b*
k	(*c* represents either the _____ or the *s*. It has no phoneme of its own, therefore no key symbol.)	
	d as in *doll.*	2. *d*
gh *ph*	*f* as in *far.* (This phoneme is sometimes spelled _____ as in *enough,* or _____ as in *graph.*)	3. *f*
hard *a* *o, u*	*g* as in *go.* (This is called the (soft, hard) sound. It is the sound usually heard when followed by the vowels _____, _____, and _____ and when followed by any other consonant or appearing at the end of the word.)	4. *g*

he	h as in (*ghost, he, honor*)	5. *h*
e, i, y	j as in *jam.* (This phoneme is often represented by a *g* followed by the vowels _____, _____, or _____.)	6. *j*
a, o, u q	k as in *kid.* (This phoneme is often represented by a *c* followed by the vowels _____, _____, or _____. It is also represented by a _____ as in *queen.*)	7. *k*
	l as in *lot.*	8. *l*
voiced	m as in *man.* This is a (voiced, voiceless) nasal sound.	9. *m*
not	n as in (*condemn, not*).	10. *n*
pan	p as in (*graph, pan*)	11. *p*
k	(*q* has no key symbol. The dictionary always uses a _____ to indicate its pronunciation.)	
	r as in *run.*	12. *r*
sat	s as in (*his, sure, sat*). (Select the word in which the *s* represents its key symbol phoneme.)	13. *s*
	t as in *tan.*	14. *t*
w	(*u* sometimes serves as the consonant _____. This is generally true when it follows *q.*)	
	v as in *van.*	15. *v*
we	w as in (*two, why, we, who*).	16. *w*
	(*x* has no phoneme of its own. It has the sound represented	
ks	by the voiced *gz*, the voiceless _____, or the *z.*)	
yes	y as in (*yes, day*).	17. *y*
	z as in *zero.*	18. *z*

A Review Of The Phonemes 87

		Key Symbols
	B. Represented by consonant digraphs	
chair (The other two have symbols *k* and *sh*.)	*ch* as in *(chair, character, machine)*.	19. *ch*
f	(*gh* has no phoneme of its own. It is often represented by the key symbol _____ as in *enough*.)	
sing	*ng* as in *(congest, sing)*.	20. *ng*
f	(*ph* has no phoneme of its own. The key symbol _____ commonly represents the sound, as in *phone*.)	
ship	*sh* as in *(ship, division)*.	21. *sh*
thin	*th* as in *(thin, Thomas)*.	22. *th*
that	*th* as in *(think, that)*.	23. t͟h
why	*wh* as in *(who, why)*.	24. *wh*
pleasure (*Edge* has the *j* key symbol.)	*zh* as in *(pleasure, edge)*.	25. *zh*

II. VOWEL PHONEMES

A. Represented by single vowel letters

	1. Long sounds	
lake	*a* as in *(lake, cat)*.	26. $\bar{a}$
me	*e* as in *(fed, me)*.	27. $\bar{e}$
ice	*i* as in *(ill, ice)*.	28. $\bar{\imath}$
no	*o* as in *(no, not)*.	29. $\bar{o}$
use	*u* as in *(use, us)*.	30. $\bar{u}$
$\bar{\imath}, \breve{\imath}$	(*y* has no vowel phoneme of its own. Its key symbol can be the _____ as in *my*, the _____ as in *myth*, and perhaps also	
long	the _____ *e* as in *happy*.)	
	2. Short sounds	
an	*a* as in *(date, an, all)*.	31. $\breve{a}$
fed	*e* as in *(fed, pine)*.	32. $\breve{e}$
pin	*i* as in *(pin, pine)*.	33. $\breve{\imath}$

hot	o as in (orb, hot).	34. ŏ
cup	u as in (cup, full).	35. ŭ
short i	y, as a vowel, has no distinctive sound of its own. It can have the key symbol of the _____ _____ as in hymn.	

3. Other single vowel sounds

a	ə represents the soft, unaccented sound of the vowel _____	36. ə
e, i, o	in comma, _____ in label, _____ in pupil, _____ in button,	
u	_____ in circus.	

dare, chair, there	â as in dare, chair, there . . . (All of these and those following are examples; underline the parts that represent the sounds.	37. â
father, hearth, sergeant	ä as in father, hearth, sergeant . . .	38. ä
order, tall, fault	ô as in order, tall, fault . . .	39. ô
hurt, term, courage	û as in hurt, term, courage . . .	40. û

B. Represented by diphthongs

	oi as in oil. This phoneme is also represented by the letters	41. oi
oy	_____ .	
	ou as in house. This phoneme is often represented by the	42. ou
ow	vowels _____ .	

C. Represented by digraphs (vowel)

food	o̅o̅ as in (food, flood).	43. o̅o̅
hook	o̅ŏ as in (food, flood, hook).	44. ŏŏ
	The key symbols for other vowel digraphs, such as ai, oa, and so forth, have already been given.	

44	Take another look at the key symbol column on these last pages.
	We have accounted for the _____ phonemes with which we are concerned in teaching reading! They may be represented by other spellings— but these are the basic sounds of the American-English language.
	Now review the headings of the outline just given.

V. Syllabication and Accent

unit, pronunciation	1. The syllable is the unit of pronunciation. It is convenient to use one-syllable words to illustrate the vowel and consonant phonemes because a one-syllable word is, in itself, a _____ of _____ .
syllable	2. The generalizations which apply to a one-syllable word may apply to each syllable of a two-or-more syllable word and generally apply to the accented _____ of a word.
syllable	3. There is one vowel phoneme in each unit of pronunciation, that is, in each _____ .
vowel two	4. Each syllable contains only one _____ phoneme. If you hear two vowel phonemes, you may be sure the word has _____ syllables.
phoneme *pine* ī *boy* oi *right* ī *pause* ô (If you missed *pause* ô, reread the frame.)	5. Each syllable may have more than one vowel letter but only one vowel _____ . The word *cause (kôz)* has one vowel phoneme: ô. Underline the vowel letters in the words at the right. Write the key symbol which represents the vowel phoneme in the space following each word; mark it to show pronunciation. *pine* _____ *boy* _____ *right* _____ *pause* _____

syllables	6. How many units of pronunciation (or _____) are there in these words? What is the vowel phoneme in each syllable? Mark the vowel(s), in the space at the right, to show pronunciation.

			No. of Syllables	Vowel Phoneme(s)
1	ĕ		red _____	_____
1	ŭ	(jŭmpt)	jumped _____	_____
2	ă	ĭ (or ə)	candid _____	_____
2	ā	ĭ	raining _____	_____
1	ou		house _____	_____

syllable	7. One syllable in a two or more syllable word receives more emphasis or greater stress than the other syllables. We indicate this accented _____ by placing an accent mark (') at the end of the accented syllable.
accent (or stress)	8. In multisyllabic words, more than one syllable may be stressed. There will be one primary _____ (shown by ') and one or more secondary accents. The secondary accent is shown by '.
vowel	9. We have already noted that accent, or stress, affects _____ (vowel, consonant) sounds.
accented	10. The vowel phoneme is the most prominent part of the syllable. Vowels behave differently in accented and unaccented syllables. The vowel is most clearly heard in the _____ syllable.
schwa	11. Many syllables, when pronounced carefully in isolation, appear to follow the generalizations we have noted. In normal speech, however, we have a tendency to give most vowels in the unaccented syllables the soft, short, indistinct _____ sound.
ŏ ə	12. We can clearly see this behavior of vowels in accented and unaccented syllables in words which are spelled alike but accented differently. Read these sentences: *Your <u>conduct</u> is exemplary. (k _____ n'dukt)* *I will <u>conduct</u> you through the factory. (k _____ n dukt')* Show the pronunciation of the vowel in each of the first syllables above.

kŏn′	13. Write the first syllable of each of the underlined words to show its pronunciation. If the first syllable is the stressed syllable, include the accent mark.
kən	*I signed the contract.* _____
kəm	*"Can't" is a contraction.* _____
kŏm′	*The work is complete.* _____
	You are competent! _____
phoneme	14. Each syllable has only one vowel _____ . It may have more
	(phoneme, letter)
letter	than one vowel _____ .
	(phoneme, letter)
yes	15. Is *boy* a one-syllable word? _____ Does it have more than
yes	one vowel letter? _____ Does it have one vowel phoneme?
yes, *oi*	_____ What key symbol represents this phoneme? _____ This
diphthong	vowel phoneme is called a _____ .
	16. To decode a word not known at sight, we need to have some idea of where to place the accent.
accent	There are some clues to where the _____ may be found in unknown words.

Clues to Placement of Accent

accent	1. Obviously, it is necessary to have some understanding of where to expect to find the accented syllable. First, we consider one-syllable words to have a primary _____ .
yes (They are one syllable words, therefore they are the accented syllable.)	2. The vowel phoneme in the accented syllable tends to follow the generalizations we have studied concerning its sound. *met* *rain* *rate* Would you expect the words at the right to conform to these generalizations? _____ *cat* *hope* *boy*
accented	3. Dictionaries, in showing pronunciation, do not place accent marks on one-syllable words. It is taken for granted that they are _____ .

chang' vest' pay' fine'	4. In general, prefixes and suffixes (affixes) form separate syllables. The accent usually falls on or within the root word. Place the accents in these words. *ex chang ing* *in vest ment* *pay ment* *re fine ment*
suffix	5. The root word is more likely to be accented than the prefix or _____ .
accent see'saw frame'work black'bird	6. In compound words, the primary _____ usually falls on or within the first "word." Rewrite these compound words to show the syllables; place the accents. *seesaw* _____ *framework* _____ *blackbird* _____
   black bird' black'bird	7. Accent within sentences will not be considered here. However, note that a change in accent in the following sentences changes the meaning. Place the accent on *black* or *bird* in each sentence: *I see a black bird; I think it is a crow.* *The blackbird built its nest in the marsh.*
root first	8. We have noted that (1) one-syllable words are accented; (2) accents usually fall on or within the _____ word rather than on an affix; (3) the _____ "word" in a compound word is usually the accented one.
first second first second nouns	9. The place of the accent may differentiate between a noun and a verb in words that are spelled alike: What is this <u>object</u>? _____ Do you <u>object</u>? _____ This is a <u>present</u> for you. _____ Please <u>present</u> this to your friend. _____ The accents fall on the first syllables in the _____ in the above (What part of speech?) sentences. Write <u>first</u> or <u>second</u> to show the syllable on which the accent falls in each of the underlined words.
be gin'ning mil'lion fet'ter	10. When there is a double consonant within a word, the accent usually falls on the syllable which closes with the first letter of the double consonant: *lat'ter.* Place the accents in these words. *be gin ning* *mil lion* *fet ter*

dec la ma'tion dec la ra'tion ex ag ger a'tion grav i ta'tion	11. In most multisyllabic words ending in *tion,* the primary accent falls on the syllable preceding the *tion* ending. Example: *del e ga' tion.* Place the primary accents in these words.	dec la ma tion dec la ra tion ex ag ger a tion grav i ta tion
main tain' con ceal' com plain'	12. When the vowel phoneme in the last syllable of a word is composed of two vowel letters, that syllable is most often accented. Mark the accents in these words.	main tain con ceal com plain
first consonant vowel tion	13. We have noted that (1) when a word is used as different parts of speech, the accent is usually on the _____ syllable of the noun; (2) the accent usually falls on the syllable which closes with the first letter of a double _____; (3) when the last (and closed) syllable of a word has two _____ letters, that syllable is accented; and (4) the accent falls on the syllable preceding the _____ ending.	
o'men prac'tice scoun'drel cen'ter mon'key glis'ten	14. When there is no other clue in a two-syllable word, the accent most often falls on the first syllable. Study these words to see if they follow this generalization. Place the accents.	o men prac tice scoun drel cen ter mon key glis ten
accented	15. Let's review all the generalizations concerning the placement of the accent. Consider the word *dance.* A one-syllable word is considered to be _____. (accented, unaccented)	
sun'set compound, first	16. Rewrite the word *sunset* and place the accent: _____. In _____ words, the accent usually falls on the _____ "word."	
re source'ful root prefix	17. Rewrite the word *resourceful* and place the accent: _____. The accent usually falls on the _____ word rather than on the suffix or _____.	

de hu mid'i fy root	18. Consider this word: *de hu mid i fy.* Sometimes a root word has more than one affix, or the word has so many syllables that two or more syllables are stressed. The primary accent, then, usually falls on or within the _____ word. Place the primary accent in the word above.
noun	19. Consider the word *rebel.* Certain words which are spelled the same sometimes function as different parts of speech. The accent on the first syllable generally indicates that it is a _____.
re gret'ta ble consonant closes consonant	20. Consider this word: *re gret ta ble.* When there is a double _____ within a word, the accent usually falls on the syllable which _____ with the first letter of the (closes, opens) double _____ . Place the accent in the word above.
cur tail' last	21. Consider this word: *cur tail.* When two vowel letters appear within the last syllable of a two-syllable word, the _____ syllable is most often accented. (first, last)
for get'ting *con' tract* *de mand'ed* *ap pear'ance* *o' pen ing* *can teen'* *show'boat*	22. Using what information you have and remembering that it is not customary to place accent marks on one-syllable words, place accent marks in all the appropriate places in the following: *I was for get ting my con tract which de mand ed my ap pear ance* *at the o pen ing of the can teen on the show boat.*

REVIEW 19

1. The unit of pronunciation is the _____ .
2. The basic speech sound, or the smallest sound-bearing unit, is the _____ .
3. Can there be more than one vowel letter in a syllable? _____
4. Can there be more than one vowel sound in a syllable? _____
5. The vowel phoneme is most clearly heard in the _____ syllable.

6. We studied several generalizations concerning the placement of accent marks. State the generalization which applies to each of these words. Place the primary accent in each word.

a. *in ter change a ble*

b. *book man*

c. *fast*

d. *ex'port; ex port'*

e. *gen er a tion*

f. *to mor row*

g. *con geal*

h. *go pher*

(See the Appendix for the answers to Review 19.)

Clues to Syllable Division

A single vowel in a closed syllable generally represents its short sound.	1. We have established some guidelines to help us decide upon which syllable an accent might fall. We still have this problem: Where do the syllabic divisions occur? There are generalizations to help but with many exceptions. First, we need to review two generalizations concerning vowel phonemes. State the generalization which applies to the vowel sound of *met.*
A single vowel in an open syllable generally represents its long sound.	2. State the generalization which applies to the vowel sound of *me* and *so.*
short (unglided)	3. Let's attempt to syllabicate the word *pupil.* If you divided it *pup il,* the first vowel would be expected to have its _____ sound.
long (glided), open	4. If you divided it *pu pil,* the first vowel would be expected to have its _____ sound: It is in a(an) _____ syllable. <div align="center">(open, closed)</div>
pu pil	5. Syllabicate *pupil* correctly: _____ _____.
When there is no other clue in a two-syllable word, the accent most often falls on the first syllable.	6. Which generalization concerning placement of accent would seem to apply?
last (unaccented) *pū´pəl*	7. Write the complete pronunciation of *pupil,* marking the accent and using the schwa in the _____ syllable. _____
pu pil (pū´pəl)	8. Now write it as it would appear in the dictionary. The entry word should show syllabication only. Follow this by rewriting the word to show pronunciation, using the key symbols and omitting silent letters (if any). _____ _____

consonant consonant vowel	9. Let us make a generalization: If the first vowel in a two-syllable word is followed by a single _____, that _____ often begins the second syllable. In other words, the syllable division is between the single _____ and the single consonant.
si lent (sī′ lənt) cro cus (krō′ kəs) lo cal (lō′ kəl)	10. Follow the above gener- _silent_ _____ _____ alization and write these _crocus_ _____ _____ words as they would appear in the dictionary—entry _local_ _____ _____ word followed by pro- nunciation.
silent	11. Let us review another generalization: When two like consonants appear together, the second is generally _____.
unglided glided, unglided	12. Examine the word _puppet._ If we divide it _pup pet,_ we would expect the first vowel to have its _____ sound. If we divide it _pu ppet,_ we would expect the _u_ to be _____. The _u_ should be _____.
closed _pŭp pet_	13. For the _u_ to have the correct sound, it should appear in a(an) _____ (closed, open) syllable. Write the word _puppet_ dividing it correctly. Mark the _u._ _____
pup pet (pŭp′ət or pŭp′ĭt) p short	14. Now write _puppet_ as it would appear in the dictionary—first the entry word, using syllabication but the correct spelling. _____ _____ (_____ _____) Follow this with the correct pronunciation. Omit the second _____. Some- times in an unaccented syllable the vowel is not a schwa but rather a related sound, the soft _____ _i._ (short, long)
consonants consonants	15. We can make a generalization: When two vowel letters are separated by two _____, the syllable division is generally between the _____.

open glided, first	16. Note the relationship between the sounds of the vowels, the syllabication, and the accent. We divided the word *pupil;* the first syllable is a(an) _____ (open, closed) syllable with the division between the vowel and the consonant. The vowel has its _____ sound, and the accent is on the _____ syllable.
closed short, first	17. Then we divided *puppet.* The first letters are the same, but the pronunciation is different: The first syllable is _____, the sound represented by the first vowel is _____, and the accent is on the _____ syllable.
closed short	18. The syllabic division between consonants is more dependable than the division between the single vowel and single consonant. There are many words in which the first single consonant ends the first syllable: *ex it, nov ice, hon or, fac et.* In these words, the first syllable is _____ and the vowel has its (open, closed) _____ sound.
second	19. When in doubt, however, try the generalization first: If the first vowel in a two-syllable word is followed by a single consonant, that consonant often begins the _____ syllable, as in *pu pil.*
tī ger yes	20. Divide *tiger* into syllables: _____ _____. Mark the vowel in the first syllable to show pronunciation. If *tiger* were spelled with two *g*'s, would it be expected to rhyme with *bigger?* _____
pĭk′chər	21. Divide *picture* into syllables. Mark the first vowel. Write the digraphs that the letters *ture* represent. Place the accent. *picture* _____ (Use key symbols for all phonemes.)
lĕt′ter yes *căn′did* yes *ĕf′fort* yes *găl′lon*	22. Study the words at the right. Is each a two- or more syllable word? _____ Is there a single vowel in the first syllable? _____ Is the single vowel followed by two consonants? _____ If so, divide the words between the consonants. Mark the first vowel in each to show its pronunciation. Mark the accent. *letter* _____ _____ *candid* _____ _____ *effort* _____ _____ *gallon* _____ _____

If the first vowel in a two-syllable word is followed by a single consonant, that consonant often begins the second syllable.	23. State the generalization for the syllabication of *meter.*
When two vowel letters are separated by two consonants, generally the word is divided between the consonants.	24. State the generalization for the syllabication of *plastic.*
hōpé *hŏp* *hŏp′ pĭng* long	25. Show the pronunciation of these words by dividing them into syllables, marking the vowels, placing the accents, and drawing a slash through silent letters. hope _____ hop _____ hopping _____ If we did not double the *p* to form *hopping,* we might expect the last letter of the first syllable to represent a _____ o. This would not be (long, short) our intention.
th	26. Remember that a two-letter grapheme, a digraph, acts as a single letter. Do not syllabicate between letters of a digraph. The word *together* is not *to get her* because the digraph _____ is not to be divided.
slŭg′ gish, rĕs′ pite *mē′ ter, lā′ ter* *mō′ tive, lăt′ ter*	27. We are studying generalizations which pertain to syllabication. In this study we are using words we already know. Now pretend you do not know the words below. Divide them into syllables following the "open-syllable, long" and "closed-syllable, short" generalizations. Mark the vowel in the first syllable to show pronunciation. Place the accent. sluggish _____ respite _____ meter _____ later _____ motive _____ latter _____
yes	28. Reread the words in the above frame. Are all of them marked the way they really are pronounced? _____ If any are not, correctly divide them into syllables and mark them.

	29. Pretend you do not know the words below. Syllabicate them according to the generalizations we've been studying. Mark the first vowel. Place the accent. Follow the directions carefully.
pī′rate, rī′gid *drā′gon, cěl′lu loid′*	pirate _____ rigid _____ dragon _____ celluloid _____
no *rĭg′id, drăg′on*	30. Reread the words in the above frame. Are they all marked the way they are really pronounced? _____. If any are not, correctly divide them into syllables and mark the vowel in the first syllable. Place the accent.
often	31. If the first vowel is followed by a single consonant, that consonant _____ begins the second syllable. (always, often) (Take time to check your results. Are you getting them all correct? Are you applying what you have learned? Do you complete a frame, writing all the answers before you move the mask down? You should be able to see the results of your study. May you have a great feeling of self-satisfaction!)
root *syllables*	32. We have observed that the accent is generally on the _____ word rather than on the prefix or suffix. It is natural then to expect prefixes and suffixes to form _____ separate from the root word.
de lay *re lent less* *re doubt a ble*	33. Divide the words at the right into syllables. delay _____ relentless _____ redoubtable _____
lā′tĕks *pā′găn (or gən)* *dĭs kŏm měn dā′shən* *lē′gəl* *wĭn′dō*	34. Observing the generalizations, divide the words at the right into syllables and mark them to show pronunciation. Place the accents. latex _____ pagan _____ discommendation _____ legal _____ window _____

two   *ble*
         cle
         ble
	35. Examine the words *table, circle, marble.*
	
	Each of these words has _____ syllables. Write the last syllable in each word. We can show the pronunciation of these syllables as *bəl, kəl.*
	
	ta _____
	cir _____
	mar _____

consonant	36. A helpful generalization is: If the last syllable of a word ends in *le* preceded by a _____, that consonant usually begins the last syllable.
ri fle (rī′fəl)	37. Write the complete pronunciation of *rifle* as it would appear in the dictionary. _____ _____ (_____ _____)
pronunciation (Meaning is correct also.)	38. Now let's examine a word which is the same as *rifle* except for a double *f*. Read this sentence: *The stones in the river caused a riffle on the surface.* The second *f* affects the _____ of the word.
f *rif fle*	39. The last syllable in *riffle* ends with *le* preceded by the consonant _____. Show how we would divide the word. (Note that other generalizations correctly apply to these words.) *riffle*
rif fle (rĭf′əl)	40. Now write *riffle* as it would appear in the dictionary. _____ _____ (_____ _____)

whiff (rhymes with *rif*)
 	
buy (rhymes with *ri*)
	41. Select rhyming words from the list at the right. (Work carefully; don't use more of the word than the instructions tell you to.)
	
	        the first syllable in *riffle* _____
	
	        the first syllable in *rifle* _____ <div align="right">*buy*
	toy
	fell
	whiff
	Eiffel</div>

trifle
 	
piffle
	42. Select rhyming words from the list at the right:
	
	        the word *rifle* _____
	
	        the word *riffle* _____ <div align="right">*gleeful*
	trifle
	awful
	piffle</div>

long	43. We have noted that the clues to the pronunciation of a given word are a. the vowel phonemes b. the consonant phonemes c. the position of the vowel in the syllable d. the syllable accented If the vowel is the last and only letter in the syllable, it usually has its _____ sound.

consonants consonant root diphthong	**44.** Syllable divisions are most commonly made a. between two _____ (as in *latter*) b. between a single vowel and a single _____ (as in *paper*) c. between prefixes, suffixes, and _____ words. They are not made between letters representing a single phoneme; that is, between the letters of a digraph or a _____ (as *cellulo<u>id</u>*).
syllable consonant	**45.** We have seen that syllables are units of pronunciation. The arrangement of vowels and consonants within the _____ affects the pronunciation. While _____ letters cannot often be pronounced in isolation, a (consonant, vowel) syllable is always a pronounceable unit.
are not	**46.** We have noted that generalizations about syllabication are helpful but _____ infallible. (are, are not)
ā′bəl	**47.** Sounds may change with the lengthening of the word: Divide *able* into syllables. Mark to show pronunciation. _____
change a ble chānj′ə bəl	**48.** Divide *changeable* into syllables. _____ Rewrite to show pronunciation. _____
long schwa unaccented	**49.** In *able* the *a* represents the _____ sound. In *changeable* the second *a* represents the _____ sound; it is now in the _____ syllable. (accented, unaccented)

Cv̆C Cv̆ph
v̆C Cv̆C
blv̄ Cv̄
Cv̆ph Cv̄phé
 	
Did you succeed?
	50. To check our understanding, let's use symbols. Study the key below at the left. Divide the "words" in the right column into syllables, marking the vowels as they would be found most commonly and as though all syllables were accented.
	
	Key: C is <u>c</u>onsonant
	          v is <u>v</u>owel (other than *e*) é is silent *e*
	          ph is di<u>g</u>raph
	          bl is <u>bl</u>end
	
	                        C v C C v ph
	                        v C C v C
	                        bl v C v
	                        C v ph C v ph é

REVIEW 20

1. Examine the following consonant-vowel word patterns. Place a slash where the syllable division would be most likely to occur. Make sure that there is a vowel in each syllable. Give the reason you divided the word as you did. There are no digraphs in these words.

   a. CVCVCC

   b. CVCCVC

   c. CVCCV

   d. CCVCVCC

2. How would you expect the following words to be divided? Why? (Pretend that you do not know the words; then you cannot say, "I can hear the pronunciation unit.")

   a. *respectful*

   b. *capable*

   c. *father*

(See the Appendix for the answers to Review 20.)

After you have corrected Review 20, take the posttest found on the following pages.

Self-evaluation II: A Posttest

This test is designed to help you evaluate your growth in the field of phonics. Read each item, including all choices. Indicate the answer you consider best by circling the appropriate letter (a, b, c, d, or e) or by marking the appropriate letter on an answer sheet. Please respond to every item. Time: 30 minutes.

I. Multiple Choice. Select the best answer.

1. Which of the following most adequately completes the sentence? All the consonant phonemes in the English language are represented by
   a. the consonant-vowel combinations.
   b. the distinctive speech sounds we associate with each of the 21 consonant letters of the alphabet.
   c. 18 of the consonant letters of the alphabet plus seven digraphs
   d. the single-letter consonants plus their two- and three-letter blends.
   e. the English language is too irregular to represent the consonant phonemes with any degree of accuracy.

2. The second syllable of the nonsense word *omethbin* would be expected to rhyme with
   a. see.   b. pet.   c. wreath.   d. breath.   e. kin.

3. The open syllable in the nonsense word *phattoe* would be expected to rhyme with
   a. *fa* of *fatal.*   b. day.   c. row.   d. a. and b.   e. None of these

4. How many phonemes are represented in the nonsense word *ghight?*
   a. one   b. two   c. three   d. four   e. six

5. The sound of the schwa is represented by
   a. the *a* in *carry.*
   b. the *e* in *lemon.*
   c. the *i* in *lighted.*
   d. the *o* in *falcon.*
   e. None of these

6. A diphthong is best illustrated by the vowels representing the sound of
   a. *oo* in *foot.*
   b. *oy* in *employ.*
   c. *ow* in *low.*
   d. *ai* in *said.*
   e. All of the above

7. Generally, when two like-consonants appear together in a word
   a. one is sounded with the first syllable and the other with the second.
   b. both are sounded when the preceding vowel is *e.*
   c. both are sounded when the following vowel is *i.*
   d. only one is sounded.
   e. neither is sounded.

8. A requirement of a syllable is that
   a. it contain no more than one vowel letter.
   b. it contain no more than one vowel phoneme.
   c. it contain at least one consonant phoneme.
   d. it contain no more than one phoneme.
   e. None of the above.

9. An example of a closed syllable is
   a. low.
   b. dough.
   c. doubt.
   d. All of these
   e. None of these

10. The letter *y* is most likely to be a consonant when
    a. it follows *o* in a syllable.
    b. it has the sound of *i* as in *light.*
    c. it is the first letter in a word or syllable.
    d. it is the last letter in a word or syllable.
    e. None of the above

11. The letter *q* could be removed from the alphabet because it could adequately and without conflict be represented by
    a. *ch* as in *choir.*
    b. *k* as in *kite.*
    c. *cu* as in *cubic.*
    d. All of the above
    e. The idea is foolish; *qu* represents a distinctive consonant phoneme.

12. An example of an open syllable is found in the word
    a. bough.
    b. replay
    c. do.
    d. All of these
    e. None of these

13. Which of the following has the incorrect diacritical mark?
    a. băll   b. fĕll   c. wĭsh   d. drŏp   e. cŭt

14. Which of the following has an incorrect diacritical mark?
    a. spāde   b. rēady   c. insīde   d. lōne   e. fūse

15. When *o* and *a* appear together in a syllable, they usually represent the same sound as
    a. the *o* in *crook.*
    b. the *o* in *done.*
    c. the *o* in *force.*
    d. the *o* in *ghostly.*
    e. None of these

16. The symbol *s* is used in the dictionary to show the pronunciation of the sound heard in
    a. should.   b. has.   c. sure.   d. zoo.   e. None of these

17. If *e* were the only vowel in an open syllable, that *e* would most likely represent the same sound as
    a. the *y* in *by.*
    b. the *ea* in *seat.*
    c. the *e* in *get.*
    d. the *e* in *fine.*
    e. None of these

18. The consonant blend is illustrated by
    a. the *ch* in *chin.*
    b. the *ng* in *sing.*
    c. the *bl* in *black.*
    d. the *ph* in *graph.*
    e. a., c., and d.

19. When the single vowel *i* in an accented syllable is followed by a single consonant and a final *e*, the *i* would most likely have the sound of
    a. the *i* in *readily.*
    b. the *i* in *active.*
    c. the *y* in *cry.*
    d. the *e* in *sea.*
    e. None of these

20. If *a* were the single vowel in an accented syllable ending with a consonant, that *a* would most likely represent the same sound as
    a. the *ay* in *daylight.*
    b. the *ai* in *plaid.*
    c. the *a* in *many.*
    d. the *a* in *wall.*
    e. None of these

21. When *c* is followed by *i*, it is most likely to represent the same sound as
    a. the *c* in *cube.*
    b. the *c* in *chime.*
    c. the *c* in *cello.*
    d. *c* followed by *o.*
    e. None of these

22. The word *if* ends with the same sound as
    a. the *ph* of *phrase.*
    b. the *f* in *of.*
    c. the *gh* in *cough.*
    d. All of the above
    e. a. and c.

23. The symbol *w* is used in the dictionary to show the pronunciation of the sound heard in
    a. want.　　b. now.　　c. who.　　d. two.　　e. a., b., and c.

24. When the letter *g* is followed by *a*, it most likely will represent the same sound as
    a. the *j* in *jam.*
    b. the *g* in *ghastly.*
    c. the *g* followed by *u.*
    d. the *g* in *bring.*
    e. Both b. and c. above

II. Complete each sentence by selecting the word for which the correct pronunciation is indicated.

25. When I picked my vegetables, I dropped a
    a. kô′lə flou′ ər　　b. kăr′ŏt　　c. kŭ kŭm′bĕr　　d. pē　　e. ŭn′ĭən

26. I went to the park for a
    a. kŏn′cûrt　　b. rās　　c. wòlk　　d. pĭk′nək　　e. pär′tē

27. The wall is
    a. thĭn　　b. stŭck′o̯od　　c. kŏng′krĕt　　d. pĕb′bəld　　e. krăk′əd

28. The tree we planted was a
    a. fĭr　　b. sȳ′prəs　　c. spro͞os　　d. bərtch　　e. cē kwoi′ə

29. I went to the grocery story for
    a. ôr′ĭng əz　　b. brēd　　c. jăm　　d. ko͞ok′ēz　　e. kăn′dȳ

30. The committee was composed of
    a. pi′ləts　　b. fĭz′əsĭsts　　c. pə′lac　　d. mū sĭzh′ənz　　e. ô′ŧħərz

III. Multiple Choice. Where does the accent fall in the words or nonsense words given at the left? Indicate your answer by selecting the last two letters of the accented syllable found in the same row as the word.

Look at the example: *showboat.* The first "word" in a compound word is generally accented: *show′boat.* Look for the last two letters of *show, ow,* in the row to the right. You would circle b. or mark b. on your answer sheet.

Example:
showboat　　a. ho　　(b.) ow　　c. bo　　d. at

31. tenlaim　　　a. te　　b. en　　c. nl　　d. la　　e. im

32. grottome　　a. ro　　b. ot　　c. to　　d. om　　e. me

33. inligherly　　a. in　　b. nl　　c. gh　　d. er　　e. ly

34. pnight   a. pn b. ni c. ig d. gh e. ht

35. damapantion a. am b. ma c. pa d. an e. on

36. present (verb) a. re b. es c. se d. nt

IV. Multiple Choice. Select the word in each row which is <u>incorrectly</u> syllabicated.

37. a. li ly   b. li lac   c. fa tal   d. ma trix   e. lu rid

38. a. fin ger   b. cot ton   c. drun kard d. for get   e. pas tel

39. a. par don a ble b. re sist i ble c. in dent ion d. in fu sion e. ex hale

40. a. saw dust b. to get her   c. side walk d. shark skin e. loop hole

V. Multiple Choice. There are three "words" in each item (a, b, c). Select the word or nonsense word in which you would hear the same sound as that represented by the underlined part of the word at the left. You may find that the sound is heard in all three words; if so, mark d. If none of the words contain the sound, mark e.

Nonsense words (indicated with asterisks) follow the generalizations of phonics or the common pattern.

41. ten<u>t</u>   a. missed b. listen c. catch d. All e. None

42. plea<u>su</u>re a. vision b. sabotage c. rouge d. All e. None

43. ta<u>n</u>ker a. banner b. singer c. nally* d. All e. None

44. <u>g</u>em   a. edge   b. soldier c. jelly d. All e. None

45. <u>th</u>at   a. bath   b. theory c. this   d. All e. None

46. <u>ch</u>ief   a. chute   b. chord c. question d. All e. None

47. h<u>oo</u>k   a. pool   b. moose c. tooth d. All e. None

48. <u>a</u>ce   a. pac*   b. said   c. baccor* d. All e. None

49. n<u>ow</u>   a. snow   b. joyous c. cow d. All e. None

50. <u>so</u>   a. focot* b. minc* c. emcy* d. All e. None

(See the Appendix for answers to Self-Evaluation II)

Self-Evaluation II: Number correct _____

Self-Evaluation I: Number correct _____

Appendix

Definitions*

Accented syllable—Syllable which receives greater stress than the other syllables in a word. p. 91

Breve—A diacritical mark (˘) used to indicate the short (unglided) sound of a vowel. p. 64

Closed syllable—Syllable which ends with a consonant phoneme. p. 60

Consonant blend—A combination of two or more consonant phonemes blended together. p. 51

Digraph—A grapheme composed of two letters which represent one speech sound (phoneme). Consonant digraph: _cheek;_ vowel digraph: _foot._ p. 25; p. 81

Diphthong—A single vowel phoneme resembling a "glide" from one sound to another (as in _coin, house)._ p. 79

Grapheme—The written symbol used to represent a phoneme. It may be composed of one or more letters, and the same grapheme may represent more than one phoneme. (The 26 letters of the alphabet and various combinations of them form 251 graphemes which represent the 44 phonemes.) p. 8

Macron—A diacritical mark (¯) used to indicate the long (glided) sound of a vowel. p. 57

Open syllable—Syllable which ends with a vowel phoneme. p. 60

Phoneme—The smallest unit of sound which distinguishes one word from another. p. 7 This program identifies 44 phonemes. pp. 86-90

Syllable—The unit of pronunciation. There are as many syllables in a word as there are separate vowel sounds; there is only one vowel phoneme in a syllable. p. 90

*The number following each entry refers to the page on which the word was introduced.

Phonics Generalizations

CONSONANT GENERALIZATIONS

1. A letter may represent more than one phoneme. p. 13

2. A phoneme may be represented by more than one letter. p. 13

3. A letter may represent no phoneme, that is, it may be silent. p. 48

4. When two like consonants appear together, the second usually represents no sound (silent). p. 48

5. When the letter *c* or *g* is followed by *e, i,* or *y,* it usually represents its soft sound as in *city* or *gem;* when *c* or *g* is followed by any other letter or appears at the end of a word, it usually represents its hard sound as in *cup* or *go.* p. 28

6. The suffix *ed* usually forms a separate syllable when it is preceded by *t* or *d.* When the *ed* forms a separate syllable, the final *d* represents the sound associated with the key symbol *d.* p. 24

7. When the *ed* does not form a separate syllable, the final *d* represents the sound associated with the key symbol *d* if a voiced consonant precedes the *ed (stabbed),* or the sound associated with the key symbol *t* if a voiceless consonant precedes the *ed (hoped).* p. 24

VOWEL GENERALIZATIONS

1. A letter may represent more than one phoneme. p. 56

2. A phoneme may be represented by more than one vowel letter. p. 56

3. A letter may represent no phoneme, that is, it may be silent. p. 48

4. When a one-syllable word or accented syllable contains two vowels, one of which is a final *e,* the first vowel usually represents its long sound and the final *e* is silent. p. 58

5. A single vowel in an open accented syllable often represents its long sound. p. 61

6. A single vowel in a closed accented syllable usually represents its short sound. p. 68

7. When *i* is followed by *gh* or when *i* or *o* is followed by *ld,* the vowel usually represents its long sound. p. 69

8. If the only vowel letter in a word or syllable is followed by *r,* the vowel sound will be affected by that *r.* p. 75

9. If the only vowel in a word or syllable is an *a* followed by *l* or *w,* the sound of the *a* is usually that heard in *tall.* p. 78

10. When two vowel letters appear together in a one-syllable word or in an accented syllable, the first vowel often represents its long sound and the second is silent. This holds true most often for *ai, oa, ee, ey, ay* combinations. p. 81

11. Each vowel letter may represent the soft schwa sound often heard in the unaccented syllable. p. 71

ACCENT CLUES

1. The accent usually falls on or within the root word of a word containing a prefix or a suffix. p. 93

2. The accent usually falls on or within the first word of a compound word. p. 93

3. In a two-syllable word that functions as either a noun or a verb, the accent is usually on the first syllable when the word functions as a noun and on the second syllable when the word functions as a verb. p. 93

4. When there is a double consonant within a word, the accent usually falls on the syllable which ends with the first letter of the double consonant. p. 93

5. In multisyllabic words ending in *tion,* the primary accent falls on the syllable preceding the *tion* ending. p. 94

6. When the vowel phoneme within the last syllable of a two-syllable word is composed of two vowel letters, that syllable is usually accented. p. 94

7. When there is no other clue in a two-syllable word, the accent most often falls on the first syllable. p. 94

SYLLABIC DIVISION

1. In a compound word, the syllabic division usually comes between the words of which it is composed. p. 93

2. Prefixes and suffixes usually form separate syllables from the root word. p. 93

3. If the last syllable of a word ends in *le* preceded by a consonant, that consonant usually begins the last syllable. p. 102

4. If the first vowel in a two-syllable word is followed by a single consonant, that consonant often begins the second syllable. p. 98

5. When two vowel letters are separated by two consonants, the syllabic division usually occurs between the consonants. p. 98

6. In syllabication, diphthongs and digraphs are treated as representing single phonemes. p. 100

Answers to Self-Evaluations

I. Pretest

1. c	6. d	11. d	16. c	21. a	26. e	31. e	36. b	41. b	46. d
2. b	7. b	12. a	17. a	22. e	27. d	32. e	37. a	42. b	47. e
3. a	8. c	13. d	18. e	23. b	28. d	33. b	38. c	43. c	48. b
4. a	9. c	14. b	19. d	24. b	29. d	34. a	39. d	44. c	49. b
5. c	10. d	15. d	20. b	25. b	30. b	35. c	40. d	45. c	50. c

II. Posttest

1. c	6. b	11. b	16. e	21. e	26. b	31. e	36. d	41. a	46. c
2. d	7. d	12. d	17. b	22. e	27. a	32. b	37. a	42. d	47. e
3. c	8. b	13. a	18. c	23. a	28. c	33. c	38. c	43. b	48. e
4. c	9. c	14. b	19. c	24. e	29. c	34. e	39. c	44. d	49. c
5. d	10. c	15. d	20. b	25. a	30. a	35. d	40. b	45. c	50. c

Answers to the Reviews

These reviews give you an indication of your mastery (or lack of mastery) of the material. WORK TO ACHIEVE 100% ON EACH REVIEW! Your success depends largely on your self-motivation. It takes very little more effort to achieve mastery than to fail, even while writing each answer. The difference depends on your mind-set. Reread the section TO THE STUDENT. Good luck!

REVIEW 1

You should have all the answers correct. If you miss any, study the appropriate section again.

1. no   2. phonemes (The key symbols represent <u>sounds</u>, never letters.)   3. *m*   4. *m*
5. 2   6. letters   7. silent

REVIEW 2

1. *s*   2. *z*   3a. *s, sh, z, zh; z, s, zh*   3b. *c, sc; z, s, x* (any two of these)
4a. graphemes, phoneme   4b. phonemes, grapheme   5a. *van*   5b. *v, v, wolf; wolves*
5c. *buff*   5d. *of*   5e. *gh, ph*   6. *enouf, belief, very, ov, huf, beliefs, believez, books,*
zonez, fallz

Congratulations to you if you had the answers correct. If you didn't, it may be a signal to you to read more carefully. Stop to analyze the problem. Perhaps you've been working too long.

REVIEW 3

1. yes   2. *fabap, zaabz, baps*   3. *z, zaabs*   4. silent   5. *ed*   6. *d*   7. *t, d, t, d*

Youhad them all correct? Congratulations!

REVIEW 4

1. *karakter, skoolz, egz, koat, lak, gosts, antik (or antikue), seiling*   2. *g, ch, j, k; j, k, k, k*
3. *k, ch, j, k; g, j, n, s*   4. *s, i*   5. *g, o*   6. *g*   7. no

REVIEW 5

1. digraph   2. *k, k, h, zh, wh, t̶h̶; wh, ch, th, w, t̶h̶, sh; sh, g, w, sh, v, zh, r; t̶h̶, z, v, th, v, n*
3. *wea<u>th</u>er, <u>wh</u>ich, wi<u>sh</u>, bo<u>th</u>, <u>th</u>rough* (If you omitted the *wh* of *which*, you are correct, also.)

REVIEW 6

1. *m, n, ng*, voiced   2. *ng*   3. *n*   4. *m* (silent *n*)   5. *n*   6. digraphs   7. *ranje,*
ra<u>ng</u>kle, ransom; manjer, ma<u>ng</u> gle, li<u>ng</u>ks   8. *e, i, y*   9. digraph, *go, j*, silent

REVIEW 7

1. *ng (chording), wh (white), zh (measure), th̸ (there), sh (photoflash), ch (blanch)*   2. *breath*
3. (1)—(*l* is silent), (2) *yes,* (3) *sat,* (4) *tan,* (5) *jam,* (6) — (7) — (8) — (9) *van,* (10) *go,* (11) — (12) —
(13) — (not a consonant), (14) *run,* (15) *lot,* (16) *run*   4. is not, does not   5. consonant
(How did you do? You can feel a <u>real</u> sense of accomplishment if you had all of these correct. They are not easy!)

REVIEW 8

1. letter, 7, digraphs, *sh, ch, wh, zh, th, th̸, ng*   2. *gh* in *tough, ch* in *chloroform, ph* in *phoneme*
3. *f, k, f*   4. *th̸ereov, fotograf, thingk, alfabet, feazant, kouf*

REVIEW 9

1a. *e, i, y, k, a, o, u*   1b. *k*   1c. *gz, ks, z*   2a. hard *a, o, u*   2b. soft *j, e, i, y*
3a. *some, z*   4. *d, t*   5. *v*

REVIEW 10

1a. *b, d, f, g, h, j, k, l, m, n, p, r, s, t, v, w, y, z*   1b. digraphs *sh, ch, wh, zh, th, th̸, ng*
2. C has no distinctive sound of its own. It is represented by the *s* and *k*.   3. *q, x*   4. *Ph* is
represented by *f*.   5. *holesale, hi, kwik, faryngks, holy, zefyr, thach, sykik, taut, depo, glisen, dauter, rusle, dout, not, midjet, rap, super*

REVIEW 11

1. You hear the sounds represented by the letters in the blend; a digraph represents a new sound.
2. The blends are represented by phonemes we already know.   3. *bl (black), fr (freight),*
tr (train), tr (tracks)   4. *th̸ (the) ck (black), dg (nudge), th̸ (these), ck (tracks)* (The *c* in *black* and *tracks* may be considered silent.)

REVIEW 12

1. *a, e, i, o, u, w, y*   2. *w, y*   3. C, V, V, C, V, C   4. consonant digraph   5. more

REVIEW 13

1. $\bar{e}, \bar{\imath}, \bar{o}, \bar{u}$ macron   2. *i, e*   3. *e* When a word or syllable has two vowels, one of which is the final *e*, the *e* is silent and the first vowel usually represents its long (glided) sound.   4. accented, long   5. end, long   6. sound (or phoneme)

REVIEW 14

1a. When there is a single vowel in a closed accented syllable, that vowel phoneme is usually short.
1b. When a word or syllable contains a single consonant letter between a single vowel and a final *e*, that vowel usually represents its long sound and the *e* is silent.
1c. When there is a single vowel in an open accented syllable, that vowel usually represents its long sound.
2. *bīté, bǐt, căn, cāné, pět, Pēté, ǔs, fūsé, pǒck, pōké*   3. *dine* C n   *tack* C k   *ledge* C j

antique C k   *watch* C ch   *table* C l   *hello* V ō   *he* V ē   *tight* C t   *enough* C f
4. *e, i, y*

REVIEW 15

1. schwa, *e*   2. It saves assigning separate diacritical marks to each vowel to indicate a phoneme all share.   3. *river*   4. *regal, handmade* or *handmaid, celebrate, carol, estimate, suspension*

REVIEW 16

1. long or glided, $\bar{a}\ \bar{e}\ \bar{\imath}\ \bar{o}\ \bar{u}$ 2. short or unglided, $\breve{a}\ \breve{e}\ \breve{\imath}\ \breve{o}\ \breve{u}$ 3. schwa, *ə, anew (ə nū)*   4. following, *r, l, w*   5. *The tall (tôll) player does not dâre to hûrt his ärm.*

REVIEW 17

1. *oi, ou*   2. vowel   3. *plow*   4. *blō, pouns*

REVIEW 18

1. long (glided), short (unglided)   2. generalization   3. schwa, syllables   4. diphthong, *ou*
5. digraphs   6. oo $\overline{oo}$zé, mōon, rŏok, glōom, brŏok, hŏod   7. mē lēpé, phā tŏg, rěl nō, phō, ŏt, dlāff, rhōos (You are to be commended if you were able to apply the generalizations to these nonsense words.)   8. 44

116   Appendix